Mugged by Seagulls

Stories Told & Lessons Learned
Around the World

MATTHEW KLEM

DEDICATION

To my daughter Megan who said I should dedicate this book to the
Thunder Turkey.
ALL HAIL THE THUNDER TURKEY!

Table of Contents

Preface

It was a Friday afternoon, and Scott and I were at the airport. I had been shadowing him all week and was anxious to get back home. After going a whole year without a cancellation, today was going to be that fateful day. The woman at the counter told me the earliest she could get me home was on Sunday. That wasn't going to cut it. I had a wake to attend that afternoon and had to be home before then. Scott suggested we drive to Toronto from Providence, Rhode Island. Despite the snowstorm, the roads seemed passable by car. The gate agent booked me a return from Toronto to Moncton for Saturday afternoon. We got in the car and made the trek to Pearson airport.

Fast-forward 12 hours, and I finally stepped into terminal 1 at Pearson airport ready to come home. That was until the Air Canada agent told me my flight was tomorrow, not today (Saturday). I nearly popped a gasket as I told her it wasn't supposed to be for Sunday. The best she could do was put me on standby for later that day. I took her offer and made my way to a hotel. I had been up all night and needed at least a few hours of shut eye.

Upon returning to the airport later that day, they gave me a standby boarding pass. When I got to the gate, they told me it wasn't likely I could get a seat but to wait and see. As frustrated as I was, I went for a walk through the airport to calm my nerves. I made my way up the escalators and wandered down towards gate 40, which was on the other side of the terminal. About halfway there, I stopped and looked up. And at that moment, something magical happened.

I had my headphones on, and as Chantal Kreviazuk's "Time" played, I looked around the airport. From the windows on the ceiling to the passengers walking by, an incredible feeling of contentment overcame me. At that moment, I realized that I had been given a gift: The gift of travel. My job was taking me on adventures to new places that I otherwise would never have experienced. I had been so obsessed and angry about my flight cancellation that everything else had blanked out. At that moment, I realized that I was fortunate to have the chance to travel.

With a deep breath in, I felt a sense of calm fall over me. One way or the other, things would work out as they should. I finished my walk and returned downstairs to an anxious gate agent. They had been paging me over the intercom for several minutes to let me know a seat had become available. The universe had decided I would get to say goodbye to my recently deceased friend after all. Boarding pass in hand, I got on the plane and made it back in time.

Since then, I have had a lot more appreciation for the

opportunities that have been given to me when it comes to travel. With inspiration from my friends and family, I decided to sit down and write out the most memorable stories from my excursions around the world. Traveling has not only exposed me to numerous new cultures, but it's given me insight into my own life. Being pulled out of your own world and dropped into another is a sure-fire way of putting things into perspective.

Whether you get to travel or not, I hope the stories you read here inspire you to look at the world differently. It certainly has changed mine.

There's Always a Story to Tell

I had just spent the better part of a day exploring the downtown area. Having never been to this part of the world, I wanted to take in as much as possible, given that I would only be here for a week. Being right there by the water, with the bridge and opera house just behind me, this was as far from home as I could get, yet somehow it seemed familiar. Having spent most of my life in the Atlantic region of Canada, being near a wharf with the smell of the ocean around was as familiar to me as the odor of hotdog carts is to a New Yorker. I sat down at a bench and looked across the quay and thought about getting something to eat but wasn't in the mood for anything too heavy. I never was a fan of sitting alone at a table in a restaurant. I always felt that the staff was somehow looking at me, feeling bad that I was dining alone. Not that I care what others think, but sometimes you just don't feel like subjecting yourself to situations where you know people are judging. When I would dine solo, I would always end up with my face buried in my phone, trying to keep myself occupied until the food came. Occasionally I'd strike up a conversation with the waitress. That usually ended with me feeling more uncomfortable as somehow in my head, I'd think I was doing something wrong. So, for this particular night, I opted for something simple, familiar, and less awkward.

I walked into the local version of a McDonald's and ordered my good ole standby meal. Sure enough, fast food here was no faster than it was back home. After waiting for what felt like forever, I collected my food and went outside. There were tables and chairs near the pier, so I sat down to enjoy my supper among the waves. The sound of the water and the birds was far more appealing than the chatter inside the restaurant. I always revel in people watching when I am in new places. I find it interesting to see that no matter where you travel to, most people, in one way or the other, are more alike than you would think. I often wonder what people are thinking and where they are going and what brought them to the same place I had come to.

I cracked open my bag and snagged a few fries as I looked around. I took my burger out and opened the wrapper. I only got about two or three bites out of the burger before the unthinkable happened. In a flash, as I turned my head to grab a napkin to wipe my face, I experienced my first true petty crime while on the road. My burger was ripped from my hand. It happened so fast, and there was nothing I could do but sit there and try to process the absurdity of what had just ensued. For a moment, I was infuriated by the fact that I was left with no supper to eat after having spent what felt like more than half an hour waiting for a burger. Then as quickly as my dinner had been stolen from me, a surge of uncontrollable laughter struck. It was this moment that would stick with me as one of the highlights of this trip.

You might wonder why someone might burst out laughing after having been mugged. Think about it. Being mugged for a "quarter pounder" alone is pretty funny. Add to the fact that it was a seagull that ripped the burger out of my hand and then tried to fly away with it; the story takes on a whole new level of hilarity. I somehow pictured a seagull character from some Pixar movie with a burger in his beak, heading towards some nest filled with little baby birds and his wife. She asks him where the food comes from, and he proceeds to tell a heroic story about how he got the food from some silly foreigner who didn't know to keep a closer eye on his meal.

I laughed, and I laughed. I laughed so hard that the people around me were starting to look at me and questioning if I was ok. I regained my composure, got up, tossed the remainder of my meal in the trash, and went for a walk. Hell, I was in Sydney, Australia, after all, and I wasn't about to waste any of my time here. I never did get back to McDonald's for another burger, so I guess the seagull won that round after all.

That one silly incident Down Under is perhaps the most telling of why I have become so enamored with travel. Australia was a place I had wanted to go to for my entire life. Since my childhood, I had three places I had wanted to visit the most: The Pyramids of Egypt, the Galapagos Islands, and Australia. Here I was in Sydney, and now I had the absolute best story to tell about that place.

Sure, I saw the famous Sydney Opera House. I did the Sydney Harbour Bridge climb. I went snorkeling at the Great Barrier Reef. I even did a boat tour and countless other tourist type things that millions do every year. But how many people can say they went all the way to Australia and got mugged by a seagull? That story sets the tone in many ways for all of the travel I have done over the years. It's not just about being able to say, "Hey, I was there!" and point out someplace on a map to your friends to tell them you've been there. It's not about taking selfies at every little spot, posting them on Instagram to try and show off to the world. What it's really about are the stories you tell about these places that matter. Making memories about some new place you visited is what stays with you after all the souvenirs and photos are gone.

When you open a photo album and look at any photo you have from your history, each picture represents a moment in time that you chose to record. The reality is however that the image itself isn't the story. The experience you had when you took the photo is. Sometimes the story is a funny anecdote about what you saw or what you experienced. Other times it's a reminder to something more serious that gave you a moment of pause. And yes, there are also those moments where nothing profound comes of it, and it is just a moment of "Hey, I was here." When you look back on those experiences, the ones that have great stories behind them are the ones that seem to have more meaning and are easier to remember.

It also makes me a little sad when I realize that the world we are in right now seems to be such that everyone is obsessed with documenting everything we do. Sometimes it's better to put the camera away and live in that moment. Life would be pretty dull if the only stories told were those of how many photos were taken or how many likes were received on a post. When a year passes, what kind of experiences will you be able to talk about if all you did was take photos and Instagram everything?

The word I am focusing on here is experiences. Countless books, movies, and TV programs always cite, "Life is a journey, not a destination." When it comes to traveling the world and seeing all that it offers, I tend to think of a variation on that same quote. "Travel is about experiences, not destinations." When I look back at all of the places I have traveled to, of course, I remember the amazing things I have seen. What stands out far more are the experiences I had while I was on the road. From elephants eating trees, sea turtles coming to life, sitting on the set of LOST, and waves crashing against my wife all stick out in my memory because of the experiences I had.

In writing about my travels, I have found myself more interested in sharing those experiences with others, rather than naming off a long list of places I have been to. No one is all that interested in hearing about the fact I've been to New York City dozens of times. What people do like hearing are the stories told about what I experienced there. Telling the story about wandering the streets of NYC, seeing a guy dressed so ridiculous that I thought to myself, "Man, that guy dresses just like Pauley Shore." Then, as I walk by this person, I give them the "head nod" that every guy has given some other guy at some point in their life; I realize it actually *was* Pauley Shore. That story always gets a smile out of everyone I tell it to. Being able to tell that story, among others, feels far more valuable than any souvenir from a gift shop.

This idea of embracing the experience of life has led me to coin a phrase that I think sums up my thoughts perfectly: *Spend your life living, not having.* With all the places I have been to, and will someday see, I don't bring home many souvenirs. Instead, I take a deep breath, and just "go for it" and experience everything I can.

This is the story of how traveling the world has changed my life for the better. And the lessons I have learned along the way.

From Fields of Wheat
to the Drop of a Dime

I was born in Edmonton, Alberta, Canada. It's a city just shy of one million people, but for me, it was my entire world. The only time I ever got to see much of anything outside the city was when my parents would pack me in the car on a Sunday, and we'd go for a drive. My dad would get on a back road somewhere and just drive aimlessly. We never really got to see much beyond many fields of farmland, but even then, I enjoyed being somewhere else. Occasionally we'd spot something of interest and slow down. Still, by far and large, it was just the blur of many fields of wheat and other grain farms along the endless backroads that all seemed to lead back to the Yellowhead Highway.

When it came to travel beyond just a country drive in my younger years, there was very little of it. The only memorable experiences I had traveling with my family as a young kid were to Banff and Jasper. We would take summer trips down towards the mountains and stay in a cabin near town. No matter how many times we went, we always ended up with the exact same building. I remember going inside and running to the same room I had slept in the last time we stayed there. It felt like our own home away from home.

During one excursion near Canmore, dad decided we should go for a drive and explore the area. He opted to take some weird back road to go for a ride, and as we were driving, we began to notice that the road kept winding and turning in as we progressed along the way. Eventually, we got along far enough that a sign said that it was recommended we turn around or proceed at your own risk. My dad wanted to continue, but my mother insisted we stop and turn around. The road went up the side of a mountain, so we stopped at the warning sign, got out, and looked around. The town was barely visible from where we were, and we stood there wondering how we had gotten so far up and away. I remember looking down on Canmore and being amazed by how far up we were, but there was also something else there that I couldn't quite put my finger on. As a kid, you don't really appreciate the beauty or scope of things until you look back on it later in life, and this was just such an occasion. I knew there was something special about looking down on the town and seeing the beauty of everything set in the mountains. Still, I just was too young to really know how to process it all.

There's a photo somewhere in an old album in my mother's

basement that shows me in a green and yellow hoodie, sitting on a rock on the edge of Lake Louise. When I took my wife out to Alberta to meet my dad and tell him he would be a new grandfather, I took a photo of her in a very similar spot. Until this very moment, I never realized that I had unknowingly re-created an image from my own childhood with my wife in my place. Unlike my childhood memories, she at least wasn't feeding candy to the squirrels.

My first experience with air travel consisted of a trip to Moncton in 1983. Mom's sister was getting married, so we flew from Edmonton to Moncton for the wedding. I've flown hundreds of times over the years, but the first time on an aircraft is always quite an experience. Add to that, taking it all the way across Canada was something else. A few years ago, my wife and I took my kids to New York City, and they experienced their first airplane ride, train ride, and subway ride all on the same day. I remember sitting on the plane with them, recalling my own first time flying and wondered if they would remember theirs when they got to be my age.

For that first trip to Moncton though, flying was something else entirely. In those days, people smoked on airplanes, and it was always a larger aircraft that took you everywhere. I remember part of the trip sleeping across three or four seats in the middle of the plane on my way to Moncton, but now you'd be hard-pressed to see a flight with more than four spots across the body. It's also rare now for kids to see the cockpit or meet the captain. Of all things I remember from that first experience on an airplane was the bright boxy orange buttons on the panel above the seats, which turned the lights on or paged the flight attendant. I once got on a flight in the US, sat down, looked up, saw the same orange buttons, and smiled. I then wondered how old the plane was and if this would be my last flight ever.

When we were in Moncton, I got comfortable with the city and even made a friend who lived across the street. There wasn't anything monumental that happened during that first trip. In fact, the things that I did take away or discover there were so small and insignificant that it seems funny to recall them now. Everything from bacon-flavored chips to sales tax and even how the traffic lights were set up seemed new and different. Shortly after the wedding, we flew back to Edmonton, and I never gave Moncton a second thought until we moved there in the summer of 1985. After that, the only travel I experienced for several years was the occasional 30-minute drive down to Parlee Beach to visit my grandparents. It wasn't until the summer after my college graduation in 1993 when the first inkling of travel struck.

Unlike most teenagers, I didn't get my driver's license when I turned 16. I got my beginners, but it expired before I got to take my road test. I never bothered to get licensed until after I turned 19. After I moved back home from college, I opted to take up my grandparent's offer of giving me a car if I got my license. A 1989 AMC Concord station wagon had been parked in my mom's backyard, and no one was driving it. This was the car that was destined to be mine. It was about as uncool as you could get. As someone who at the time really didn't care what others thought of me, I took the car and made it my own. Green with wood panel lining the sides, it was the ugliest thing you could picture, but it was mine, and I would drive it to the limits. I got three years out of that car before the frame quit, so I certainly pushed the boundaries on what old beaters can do.

In the early years of having my own transportation, I found myself picking up a few friends and just getting in the car and driving somewhere. Sometimes it was across town then up and down Main Street a few times, and other times it was to an entirely new province. On more than one occasion, we'd get in the car and drive to a new city just "to get a coffee." We went to Springhill, Nova Scotia, because we had been told it was a great place to party. We found no parties there but did manage to steal a "No Parking" sign off the back of a convenience store in Amherst. On another trip, we drove to Saint John to visit a college friend and did get a chance to party there. The party itself wasn't memorable, but the drive home and the subsequent attempt to sleep in my own bed indeed were. Most people who know me know that I've never had a single drink of alcohol, nor have I ever experimented with recreational drugs. But the folks at this party were certainly smoking something interesting because whatever was in the air seemed to affect me after we left. The drive home saw me watch the lines on the road shrink and grow and sometimes disappear entirely. Once I got home, and into bed, my sleep was thwarted by the fact that every time I opened my eyes and stared at the wall by my bed, I was sure I could see into the wall… past the paint and gyprock. It somehow seemed to be in 3D, and even parts of the drywall were moving. I was quite happy when I finally did fall asleep.

Many of these one-off trips to other cities typically came from sheer boredom. Living in a town like Moncton, there wasn't much to do when there wasn't a house party to go to. My friends and I weren't much for the club scene as we all tended to listen to the likes of Slayer & Metallica, which you never heard at a club downtown. It seemed that getting into a car and going somewhere else always seemed more interesting than driving down Main St Moncton over and over again.

During a winter weekend down in the Annapolis Valley, I began the journey home to find myself in the ditch four times during the extended return. Between the wind and snow that blew everywhere, no winter tires on my car, and constant transport trucks on the road passing (when they shouldn't be), it was a recipe for disaster. To this day, I still have a hard time driving in the winter. Just a few years ago, I took a quick trip with my son to Halifax. After passing the city limits on our way home, the car spun and skidded into the highway median after hydroplaning. The spin-out popped a hole in the tire, and we had to get it fixed. Although it spooked my son, he was a real trooper, and now it's part of a cool story we can tell people about our first weekend away as father and son.

The furthest I ever opted to go for a spontaneous trip anywhere was actually New York City. This was more than a year later, after I had gone there for the first time. When I tell this story, I've always said the point of the trip was to go get an NYC subway token (now long replaced by the Metrocard) and come home. It sounds amusing and spontaneous. And although it was a spontaneous trip, the token was never my real reason for going. Until now, I've always omitted a small part of the story. In some ways, I think it just sounded a bit too cheesy or over the top. The truth is there was a part of me that felt compelled to take someone I knew to the Big Apple just because I knew she would love it.

There was a woman I knew while I was in college, and we had dated for a while but had a bad break up. After having not spoken for several months, we reconnected and became good friends. While I was in class, I remember thinking that I really thought she would love to see NYC. Sitting at my desk, I hatched this plan to take her and two other classmates to NYC to retrieve a subway token. I told all of them; it was just something to do for fun and wanted to see if they wanted to go.

We had no responsibilities beyond our classes, and in those days, you didn't need a passport to cross the border. So sure enough, we all packed into my car and away we went. We got as far as Houlton, Maine, where the border patrol folks gave us a real hard time and insisted on searching the car. We had nothing to hide, but after we returned to the car and hit the road, one of the guys with me *insisted* that his stuffed toy he had brought with him had been violated somehow. It was funny at the time, but now it just seems creepy.

We made it all the way to NYC, parked the car, and went exploring. We actually spotted Stephen King getting into a vehicle from a fancy hotel. None of us had the guts to walk up and introduce ourselves, but I recall that someone has a photo of him getting in the car. We ventured down into the subway system, took a ride, and kept one token, and before we knew it, we were on our way back.

A stop in a motel along the way saw the four of us crash for the night. I remember thinking that it felt good to be the one who had initiated the entire thing. My lady friend never knew that the whole trip was actually just for her, and I'm glad I never told her. Unless she's reading this, she probably still has no idea that she was the reason we went. There are times where it's nice to do something for someone and to let them know you did it so appreciation can be given. However, there are also times when you can do something for someone just because you want to, and nothing else. I really just wanted her to experience NYC, and this was a unique way I could do that for her. I didn't need or want anything in return, but oddly enough, I did get something. We got married a little over a year later. We were divorced three years after that, but despite how things for us turned out, I have no regrets about that first trip we took to the city. The subway token is hanging from the rear-view mirror of my car with several other items of significance to me. Every time I look at it, I am reminded to be kind to others and to embrace being spontaneous when you can.

I have found over the years that there are people who are unlikely to be able to experience travel outside the realm of their hometown. Typically, it's because they have never tried to save money to go, or don't think they can go, or are just plain scared to go. I have found myself on more than one occasion wanting to expose people to travel. Experience a place other than their hometown because I know that sometimes people need a bit of a push to go outside their comfort zone. Once they do, they often realize how much they were missing out. I've repeated the same gesture multiple times to different people because something inside me told me that they should see some of these places. Sure, it's nice to hear a thank you and feel some of the gratitude that comes with exposing someone to the wonders of travel. For me, the real payoff is when you see another person's face light up, or their jaw drops because of a place you brought them to. It really does make a person feel like you are giving someone else something they will remember forever.

So, when it comes to this idea of just picking up and going somewhere, it's something that has been a part of me since I got that car all those years ago. Although I don't go on as many of those spontaneous trips anymore, I still feel the urge to just get up and go sometimes. There seems to be something about getting in the car, turning my music on, and going for a long drive that seems to calm me down. Having done this enough times over the years, I've established a bit of a "loop" I like to take. From my home to some of the outlining communities and back gives me enough time to enjoy being behind the wheel. I'll turn my music on and lose myself in watching the road.

Getting in a car and going somewhere gave me enough of a push to want to see other parts of the world beyond my own little corner in Atlantic Canada. Although I took that short side-trip to NYC in college, it was actually a little trip to Toronto that really got the ball rolling.

A Dream Come True

My first significant road trip will always be special to me. It was one that was filled with countless entertaining hours in a car with one of my best friends at the time.

1995 saw me working for a pizza place as a driver. It wasn't anything glamorous, but it was a steady paycheque, which allowed me to afford to have my own vehicle with a bit extra here and there. I was also able to save money when the opportunity came for me to do something a little bit extravagant. Working as a driver, I got tips and commission for each delivery I did, so over time, they added up fast. A good Saturday night would give me $100-$150 of extra cash on top of the whole whopping $5.25/hr I was making.

I had never taken any road trips that were more than four hours to drive, so I wanted to go somewhere that I hadn't been to before, and I really wanted to make sure it was a big city. I had never been to Toronto and thought that would be an excellent spot to start.

I watched a lot of MuchMusic in those days and thought visiting the official headquarters of theirs would be a nice touch.

I booked my vacation time off for early May. Shortly after that, I found out that my favorite band, Faith No More, would be performing in Toronto later that month. I quickly made changes to my vacation dates to align with the concert and then began putting my money away.

I reached out to a guy I had met through my indie music scene contacts to see if he would be able to purchase the tickets to Faith No More for me, and I would send him the money. This was before concert tickets could be easily purchased online. Before I knew it, I had two tickets to see Faith No More in Toronto on May 22nd, 1995.

My friend Dale wanted to come but didn't have a lot of money. I didn't have a lot to spare, but I also didn't want to take this trip on my own, so I told him to bring whatever money he had and that we'd figure the rest out later. That would turn out to be the best decision as having someone there with me made it a hell of a lot more fun. Dale was a smoker, so to save him a little bit of money, I bought him one carton of smokes to start him off. The box didn't last him for the whole trip, but it did go longer than we both expected. I also knew that if he didn't have any smokes at all, I might go nuts dealing with his withdrawal and end up leaving him there.

On May 18th, 1995, at 7:00 am, we left Dale's place in Moncton and headed towards Toronto.

1995 was long before the smartphone era. The idea of having a phone in your pocket to take video and photos was unheard of. I brought my film camera, and Dale suggested that we record a "log" of what we saw on the way. Since I did many band interviews in my fanzine days, I had a little cassette recorder, and we brought it with us. Every time we saw something notable, or we just wanted to have fun, we'd record a "log" on the tape. We modeled our logs after Star Trek, and I was the captain, and Dale was the first officer. Turns out the content of that tape ended up being as entertaining as anything else we saw on that trip, save for the concert. I still have the tape, and not long ago, I converted it to MP3. Listening to those log entries provided a nice flashback and a pile of good laughs. I also have one digital file which has snippets from that tape as well as others all put to music. It comes up on rotation on my iPhone once in a while, and I always smile when I hear it.

The other thing to remember about that time was that it was pre-GPS. In the days before Google Maps and dashboard navigation, you had to use a good old fashion paper map to get you from one location to another. Dale was in charge of reading the map and navigating us to where we needed to go.

Dale was unemployed, and money for me was scarce. Motels and hotels were out of the question when it came to where we would be sleeping. As it was late spring, we packed a couple of pillows, sleeping bags, and a small two-person tent in the back of my Mercury Topaz and roughed it. We also brought a cooler with a little bit of food and some drinks. Sleeping in a tent was fine as campgrounds were cheap, and we were young and didn't really care where we crashed during the wee hours.

At the time, Toronto was about an 18-hour drive from Moncton. We didn't figure we would make it all the way in one night, so we got as far as the west side of Quebec City and crashed at a campground. We woke up the next morning, and the weather was great, so we hit the road nice and early, crossing into Ontario before lunch. We made a pit stop in Kingston in hopes that we could find our college friend, Plungerman. Since we didn't know his address or phone number, we just hoped we'd see him somewhere before we continued on our way. We never did find him, but I did eventually reconnect with him via Facebook years later.

By the time we got to Toronto, we were tired. We had made the decision to stay in a campground in Whitby, just outside of the city. We got the tent put up, our stuff organized, and even though we were exhausted, we wanted to go downtown and see if we could find MuchMusic. We dug out the map, found Queen St West, got in the car, and headed into town.

I found driving there to be a lot less chaotic than I was expecting for such a large city or to see cable cars running in the main streets either. Dale spotted the MuchMusic building, so we found a parking spot and made our way there.

Now what you have to understand is that in 1995, I was 21 years old, and Dale was 22. Music was (and still is) a massive part of my life. In those days, MuchMusic was a significant source of seeing new and upcoming bands emerge onto the scene. This was in a day when MuchMusic and MTV were known primarily for playing music videos and interviewing bands, and reality TV didn't exist yet. I remember vividly being introduced to the likes of Nirvana and Pearl Jam through a TV set tuned into MuchMusic. Dale and I were both avid viewers of many of the programs that ran on that station, so for us, getting a chance to go see the main headquarters where the VJs did their stuff was kind of a big deal. At the time, it would have been the closest we would come to seeing anyone even remotely famous.

At that age, we also loved seeing pretty girls. On Friday nights, MuchMusic always ran a dance party show called Electric Circus. We made our way down Queen Street West heading towards the CHUM building. Now known as the headquarters for Bell Media, you could clearly see the jeep sticking out of the side of the second floor. We knew we were in the right place.

The place was pretty quiet, but we did spot one of their VJs coming out of a store across the street, and Dale yelled out, "Hey Steve," to which Steve Anthony (a VJ for Much) waved back to us. After visiting a few other notable spots in downtown Toronto, we came back to find that Electric Circus was doing "teen" night. It seemed a bit creepy for us "old guys" to be hanging out watching teen girls, so we took off but not before spotting the super-hot VJ Monica Deol. They weren't movie stars, but we did feel kind of excited getting to see these people we recognized from TV.

Beyond that, it was just us wandering around downtown Toronto unsure of what to do with ourselves. The reality was, we really came to Toronto just for the concert and nothing else. So being downtown, it was a bit overwhelming to try and think about what we should do, with virtually no money. It was a Friday night, but we didn't really know the area, and neither of us was really into clubs. We opted for a drive to see some more stuff and then headed back to the campground.

The next day started off with us trying to find The

Warehouse, where the concert was going to be. We wanted to make sure we knew where it was ahead of time, so we'd be able to get in line nice and early on Monday afternoon. After that, we took a trip to Peterborough to visit another college friend of ours, Mary. Looking back on our visit to see her, I think we just wanted to see a familiar face. Plus, I owed her a bag of cookies.

Mary was a girl I met in 1992 during my year away at college. I had developed a bit of a crush on her. Still, nothing happened as she already had a boyfriend, but the two of us became friends. Over time, a running joke about Oreo cookies began. It started as one of those college things that just comes out of nowhere because you're bored one night, and things just happen. I'd occasionally hear someone babble something and have no idea what they had said. I'd reply with

"You did what to who in the backseat of whose car for how many double-stuffed Oreos?" I said this to Mary once, and somehow, I ended up on the hook for a bag of cookies.

So, when I knew we'd be close to where she lived, I picked up a bag of double-stuffed Oreos, and Dale and I drove to her place. She certainly got a kick out of the cookies, and we ended up hanging out there most of the day and then going to a club that night.

Now, you need to understand that Dale and I were geeks long before geeks were cool. We were into computer programming, hacking, science fiction, and plenty of other non-interesting things to different people. I mean, we used to spend hours in my basement putting lighter fluid gas into pop cans just so we could light them and see the fire shoot out the bottom. There were even times when many us would just sit around and make up stupid words only we knew the meanings for just to confuse other people. Going out bar hopping wasn't exactly on our radar. The only reason we agreed to go to the club with Mary was that she really wanted to go, and we didn't really have anything else we wanted to do. Plus, let's face it; a pretty girl wanted to take us out somewhere, so like many young straight men, we followed.

Both Dale and I agreed that the club Mary took us to was just like all other clubs: lame. The music was awful, and the only thing that was appealing about it was that we were there with Mary and that as young guys, we liked looking at the cute girls dancing. However, after a couple of hours of sheer boredom, we'd had enough and opted to bail. We decided to head back to the big city, but by the time we got near our campground, we were pretty tired. So, we both crashed, knowing we would have to pack the tent up in the morning for our next excursion.

Sunday consisted of driving to Thamesford to visit my aunt and her family. Still, before we hit the road, we made a stop at the Eaton's Centre downtown. I snapped a photo of Dale poking fun at some of the other tourists. When we got back to the car, we knew we would not be using anything left in the cooler, so we dumped it out. There was still one steak left, but it had been sitting in that cooler for a few days with very little ice. Instead of just throwing it out, we took the steak and put it under the tire of some high end, fancy car, and left it there. As I said, we were definitely different.

We got to Thamesford that afternoon and were so glad that we'd be staying in a real bed that night. However, to this day, neither Dale nor I can hear the song "Free Bird" and not think of that evening. I was thrilled to see my relatives mainly because it was rare they came out east to visit. After a few hours of hanging out, Dale and I were sitting in a room, and my uncle came out, and he was quite drunk. I mean, really drunk. He proceeded to tell us that we needed to hear some good music, so he put on "Free Bird" and turned the stereo volume up relatively high. At first, there was this horribly awful noise that came out of the speakers that sounded like a drunken dog trying to sing. I then realized that it was just the song. But then my uncle opted to crank the volume to 11, and everything became even more distorted. We just sat there, enduring this ridiculously loud music, watching my uncle headbang.

Now when I think of him that night, I think of Stan's dad Randy from the TV show South Park after he's had a few drinks and starts wailing. That was pretty much my uncle that night. We sat there waiting and wondering what we should do. It didn't feel right to just get up and leave, but we also didn't want to sit there and deal with the horribly loud, bad music and an even louder and drunk uncle. He had insisted on keeping it on repeat. Do you know how long that song is? It's even longer when you have to listen to it on repeat again, and again, and again. Eventually, we did get out of there. We went out to a local diner with my cousins, who were close to our age. We sat around talking until the early hours of the morning. The next day we got up and said our farewells, then headed back to the city to make our way to the concert.

Apart from crashing at my aunt's place, we had been sleeping in a tent mainly because it was cheap. Knowing how exhausted we would be after the show, I opted to find a motel room in Mississauga, and we dropped our stuff off there. The reality was I knew that when the concert was over, I'd want to sleep in a real bed before getting up the next morning to come home. Funny enough, Dale was so beat he fell asleep on the floor not long after we got back after the concert.

Just before we got to the venue, I stopped at a store. I bought a disposable film camera (again, pre-smartphone days), and my intention was to sneak it into the venue to snap a few photos. When we got to The Warehouse, there weren't many people there, so we were thrilled and even more so when we ultimately ended up first in line. We were even happier when the band came through the back, and we got to see them all. I got an autograph from the drummer and talked to the keyboardist whom I had interviewed for my fanzine just weeks earlier.

We had brought a bag of goodies to give the band. The swag was all of the issues of our fanzine for them to have. The 'zine was partially inspired by the band, and we really wanted to give it to them. Standing in the line, as the band members walk into the building, Dale yells out, "Puffy!" This was the nickname for the drummer, who immediately spotted Dale and came over. We handed him the bag and said, thanks. No idea if they ever looked at what was in it, but it was still pretty cool.

After sitting in line for four hours, we were let into the building and got through security. I had stuffed the camera into my pants near my crotch, and it never got discovered. We eventually got to the front of the stage and had to sit through Steel Pole Bathtub's awful set. After what felt like forever, Faith No More finally took the stage. I had seen many bands perform back home and had been excited to see shows before, but you can't possibly know how excited I was to be there.

I credit Faith No More, and their singer Mike Patton in particular, as having a substantial influence on my youth. Not just in my interest in many flavors of music, but as someone that helped me get through the awkward years of high school and college. I was exposed to drugs and alcohol through my friends but had always made a conscious decision to steer clear. Part of that came from my upbringing and dealing with two alcoholic grandparents and a mom who told me to be responsible. The other part came from reading and hearing countless stories about Mike Patton's insistence that he didn't need drugs or alcohol to do crazy stuff. Believe me, his stage antics would convince anyone he was stoned or drunk. Even his bandmates would say his only drug was sugar and that he just didn't need anything else to be wild. For some reason, this really struck a chord with me and helped bring me out of my shell.

In many ways, I emulated Patton's antics among my friends. I became known for being the guy that would pretty much do anything. It also steered me clear of a lot of crap I saw in my youth and gave birth to a hell of a lot of insane and silly experiences. So for me, seeing the band live wasn't just about going to a concert. It was about finally being able to see someone I had looked up to for so long.

I had told Dale that I really hoped they played the song Ricochet, which was my favorite tune of theirs at the time and was on the new album for which they were touring. Much to my delight, the show opened with that song. From then on, it was a non-stop intense hammering of music for the rest of the night.

Up to that point in my life, I can honestly say that nothing came even remotely close to how exhilarating that concert was to me. Anyone who knows me knows that I worshipped this band in those days and would have gone anywhere to see them. So, to finally see these guys perform live was a dream come true. Unfortunately, I had tried to get the camera out of my pants during their set. It had slid down my pant leg, and since I was basically being crushed by the crowd, there was no way I was going to get to it. I opted to say the hell with it and just enjoyed the show. They played an incredible set and joked with the crowd, and by the time the show was over, Dale & I barely had enough strength to walk to the car. I didn't care. I had seen Faith No More, met a few guys from the band and lived through the concert. How was I ever going to top that?

When the show was over, we managed somehow to get back to the motel room and basically died for the night. We needed to rest because when we got up in the morning, we had to figure out what to do about getting home.

To keep the scenery different, we decided to travel through the US. The actual travel time was considerably longer than going through Canada. Still, we wanted to see what the fuss was all about. This was when you could cross the border with just your driver's license. We left Toronto and drove to Niagara Falls and thought about stopping to see the falls but didn't see a quick and comfortable spot to park. Along the way, we paused on the bridge as we crossed into the US, Dale jumped out, snapped a few photos, got back in the car, and we kept on trucking.

We got into the US and started the drive home. The plan was to go straight through and not stop. Dale didn't have his license, so I did all the driving, and it definitely took a toll on me. We got stopped by the cops several times for a blown headlight. I explained to the police that we were just on our way back home to Canada. Having New Brunswick plates on the car certainly helped back that story as well. Thankfully, we were given a defect card by the cops that basically meant that if we got stopped again, we could just show the card and be left alone. I remember going into an Irving station in Maine and wanting to purchase a replacement headlight. The Royal Bank ATM wouldn't take my bank card. A Canadian bank in a Canadian owned gas station wouldn't accept a Canadian ATM card. I was less than happy about the situation. Not long after, we got stopped by the cops a second time. I grabbed the defect card and held it up as the cop came over. He took one look at it, thanked us for our time, and let us go. Within an hour, we had yet another cop follow us for quite a while before turning around and opting to leave us alone. We pushed towards Moncton and got to the Canadian border early in the morning around six or seven. I was exhausted, but we only had a few more hours of driving before arriving in Moncton.

The last three hours of driving eastward through New Brunswick were really hard. I was falling asleep at the wheel repeatedly, so I would roll the window down to let the wind help keep me awake. I drank countless bottles of Coke to ante up the caffeine. By the time I got to Sussex, which is only 45 minutes away from home, we took a pause at a gas station, and I half napped for about 10 minutes. We got back in the car, pointed it east, and made it home in one piece.

Now having been across the globe and back, my road trip to

Toronto still holds a special place in my heart. I think the biggest reason for that is it was my first *real* road trip. Dale and I had gone to a few other cities near home, but this was the first time we ever made a lengthy trip somewhere big. It also represented an extension of my desire to be exposed to things beyond my own borders. Sure, I had lived in a big city and had even been back to Edmonton by this point, but I was now starting to feel the urge to explore areas I had never seen before.

The entire time I drove back to Moncton, I kept thinking about how I was ever going to top that trip. At 21, watching my favorite band, led by a man I had a severe hero-worship to, it felt like I'd never beat it. As I got closer to Moncton, I finally came up with my answer about what would come next. That's when I gave myself the goal of seeing Toronto, New York City, Los Angeles, and Vancouver all before I turned 25. I could cross Toronto off that list now but had three more cities to go. Then I thought about which of those would be next, and out of nowhere, the idea of going to New York City to see a taping of David Letterman just appeared in my head. I sat on the idea as I got closer to home, and by the time I got back into my own bed and settled in for a nice nap, I was already thinking about how I could get to NYC next year.

The Empire City

Of all of the spots that I have visited in the world, New York City is one that is incredibly special to me. I have been back there repeatedly, and no matter how many times I set foot on any NYC street, it's always a welcome place for me to be.

It's the one place in the world that I have been back to repeatedly, and each time I go, there's something new that I experience there. I look forward to any chance to visit that city, and I am always looking to find an excuse to go there for something. Even after repeated visits, some experiences stand out above the rest.

The first time I set foot into NYC was in 1996. I took a road trip with my friend Cheez for the sole purpose of seeing a taping of The Late Show with David Letterman, now hosted by Stephen Colbert. I had acquired tickets to his show and booked my vacation time accordingly. We drove all the way from Moncton to Croton-on-Hudson, NY, which is a small town north of Manhattan. I was still working as a pizza delivery guy, so getting a hotel in downtown

NYC was never going to happen. I had learned the year before during my excursion to Toronto that camping in a campground outside the city then taking the train into the city made a lot more sense. For someone in his 20s who didn't care about where he slept, camping was just fine. At my age now, give me my hotel and room service. Thank you.

It's about a 14-hour drive from Moncton to New York, so when I traveled by car with Cheez for my first trip to NYC, we split the driving up between us. The actual drive to the city was not all that notable. I opted to do the "log" as I did on my trip to Toronto, and it did provide some entertaining commentary. The most surprising aspect of the actual road trip to the city had to do with one part of the route we took.

According to our map (1996, pre-Google), Croton-on-Hudson was located just off Highway 9. We would be taking exit 13 then turning onto Highway 9 South. I took the exit, paused at the stop sign, turned left, and kept rolling south. Three years later, I would exit onto that same road and pull up to the same stop sign and have a sense of familiarity. Instead of NYC, I turned right instead of left to head towards Poughkeepsie, NY. I spent a year living in that area, working as a programmer for IBM. It seems so uncanny that of all places I would have ended up moving to, I'd move to a place that I had encountered a few years earlier.

The first night we got to the campground, we were exhausted but psyched about getting to see the big city. Before we knew it, morning had arrived, and it was time to take a ride to the Big Apple.

For me, sitting on that train going into the city, I watched everything pass by. As we got closer and closer to midtown, taller buildings started to appear. And just as the surroundings seemed to be creeping in on us, the train went underground destined for Grand Central Station. A few years ago, when I took my kids to NYC for the first time, it was very much the same. We took the train from Newark Airport to Penn Station, and before we got close enough to really see anything, we went underground.

When I got off the train and walked up the stairs to the main concourse of Grand Central, I immediately recognized it from countless TV shows and movies I had seen it in. The first time I took my wife to NYC, I brought her there to show off the station for her to see. As she's taking pictures, she turns to me and says, "Do trains still run here?" A local heard her and began to chuckle just as I did. "Yes, the trains do still run here," I said with a grin on my face as she realized how funny her question sounded.

When my kids got off the train, my wife and I held their hands as we entered Penn Station. It's not as "grand" as Grand Central, but what does stand out, especially to a 5 and 7-year-old, is the massive amount of people. Coming from a city like Moncton where we barely break 100,000 people in total population, seeing that amount of moving people in either Penn or Grand is a bit of a shock.

The moment Cheez and I stepped out of Grand Central, the

first thing we did was look straight up. I have no doubt that every person who visits NYC for the first time steps out of a cab, train, bus, or car, and the first thing they do is look up at all of the buildings. You see an ocean of steel that seems to go on forever, and there's a unique smell that hits you. I remember thinking that the city smelled like a big city. A combination of food cart smell, gasoline exhaust, and a minor bit of subway air bleeding through the ground seems to fill your airways the first time you breathe in a city like that.

Years later, my two kids would live the same sense of amazement I did that first time, and they couldn't stop looking up and around at everything they saw. We stood in line and got a taxi to our hotel. As our cabbie drove through the streets, I saw the look of pure amazement on their faces as they peered into a world they had no idea even existed. Cheez and I spent a good couple of hours just walking around aimlessly, trying to take in as much as we could. We went into countless stores, explored side streets, and really did just wander from one street to another again and again. One of NYC's charms is the ability to just walk around for hours and find countless new things no matter what direction you might turn.

Again, for Cheez and me, the most significant part of our trip to NYC was all about David Letterman. The show was taped every Monday through Thursday, and we had tickets for Wednesday. We wandered down to the corner of 53rd and Broadway, where the Ed Sullivan theatre sat and took a few photographs of people standing in line for the taping that day. We popped into Rupert's Deli, which had been on the show occasionally. When it came to getting ready for the day of the taping, I had done my research on how to get the best seats.

The Ed Sullivan Theater

1697 Broadway

Between 53rd & 54th Streets, NYC

LATE SHOW

with

DAVID LETTERMAN

Wednesday, June 19, 1996

PERSONS UNDER 16 NOT ADMITTED

At the time, you needed to request tickets at least 6 months ahead of time if you expected to get them at all. I sent for my tickets and knew I would have to plan my trip around when I was scheduled to see the show. I also discovered that the tickets they send you do not guarantee you a spot in the audience. They get your foot in the door, but not much beyond that. It's first-come, first-serve. They form a line at the studio, and then give you a number on your ticket. That number represents your seat, sort of. Overall, the idea is to make sure that you are at the studio early, so you get a solid spot in line, guaranteeing you a good seat.

All the research I had done said that they start to seat you around 4pm and the show starts at 5pm. We wanted to be there early, and some of the info I had found said to be there around noon. We arrived there at 11:10 in the morning and were the first ones there. By 11:30am, another few people showed up, so we were even more thankful to have arrived when we did. By 2:30pm, a long line of impatient attendees sitting on the sidewalk had formed. Shortly after that, a page from CBS came out and got us to stand up and get in line while they numbered our tickets. They put a tiny but very happy #1 on my blue ticket. I hoped this would give me a great spot.

Turns out, it did. We got rounded up to go inside, told to take a bathroom break, and then got seated in the theatre. Cheez and I got front row seats directly in front of Dave's desk. We could not have had a better view.

They played a skit that Dave & Paul had done on a golf course, then the band played a tune or two, and then Paul introduced Dave, who came out to talk to the audience before the taping. He was thankful for the audience as he cracked a couple of jokes. He gave away a canned ham, and then as the music came up, he left the stage, and the show began.

It was weird to be sitting there. Dave did his monologue and a comedy skit of some kind that I can't really remember. James Caan was the first guest, followed by Julie White, an actress on a show called Grace Under Fire. Patti Smith was the musical guest.

The show ended, and people started to leave the theatre. We took a moment to stand there and sort of soak in what we had seen, and Cheez was just about to leave when I spoke up. Now, I hadn't told him, but in my mind, it was always my intention to try and get one of the cue cards used by Letterman for his monologue. We could clearly see the guy holding them from where we sat, so when the show was over, I told Cheez that we should go down there and ask the cue card guy for one of the cards. Sure enough, the guy was more than willing to give each of us a card, which we thanked him for. As we turned around to leave, we noticed that several other attendees had seen what we had done, and they, too, made a dash to get a card. However, much to their dismay, Cheez & I were the only ones permitted to take a card leaving the theatre. You really do need to seize the moment and just go for it sometimes. That taping would cement itself as one of my more prominent memories of NYC. However, there's so much more to see and do there.

Times Square is another one of those mystical places that people from around the world swarm to. It really doesn't matter what time of year it is; the area is always filled with people. I've been known to make my way down there and sit in one of those very

uncomfortable red chairs and just watch people. Countless tourists
are taking selfies of police officers walking their beat. A plethora of
horribly lame costumed individuals can be seen pestering the
tourists. All dressed as various movie and television characters
looking to make a few bucks from people taking photos. On my own,
I've rarely ever engaged with those folks, but my kids loved it. My
wife and I took them down one night and took a ton of photos with a
whole range of interesting individuals. Both my kids loved seeing all
the characters enough that when we returned one year later, they
both wore their own costumes in the square just to have fun with the
whole thing. You have to be very clear with whomever you take
photos with as plenty of other characters will try to photobomb or
chime in and take over and expect you to tip them. You're under no
obligation to tip them, but that is why they are out there. Many
people dressed up are obviously trying to milk it for money as their
costumes are cheaply made Halloween outfits from the Dollar Store.
Occasionally you'll see someone in a really well-made costume. For
those folks, I've never had a problem tipping for a photo.

The other notable street performers you'll find in the square
are the topless girls. During the warm months, you'll usually find a
handful of "showgirls" with very little on, and only body paint
covering up their nipples. They go after the guys trying to get photos
for tips, and I have been known to tip one or two of them before. The
first time I ever got my picture with one of them was during a work
trip that a buddy of mine came on with me. He took the photo while
the girl got a little bit closer than I was expecting. I tried to get my

friend to get his picture taken, but alas, he was a bit too shy about it. The novelty has sort of worn off, but whenever I visit NYC with someone new, it's always funny to see their reaction when they spot the girls in the body paint.

When I think about other places in NYC I've visited, there are so many great spots that come to mind like Liberty Island with the famous statue. Take my advice and don't bother taking the long walk up to the crown. You'll slowly crawl up a tiny stairwell for an hour with someone's rear end in your face (because that's how cramped it is). Save yourself the hassle and take your photos of the bay from the Staten Island Ferry. The Empire State Building is another staple of the city that you should try to do at least once. The view is pretty impressive, but, again, be prepared for long lines as you wait to go up to the top. I've done both Empire and Top of The Rock and prefer TotR simply because I thought the view was better, and there are almost no lineups since your ticket is for a specific time to go up.

Another great spot to visit is Roosevelt Island. Take the tram from 59th and 2nd over to the island and enjoy the views. You get a charming view of the city from there, and the tram ride itself is pretty awesome. It's the same tram featured in the first Spiderman movie with Tobey Maguire. There's also the FDR Four Freedoms Park on the southwestern tip of the island.

During a 12hr layover I had at Newark Airport, I took a subway into Manhattan. I went for a walk across the Brooklyn Bridge. It's an excellent experience and gives a beautiful view of the city. Plus, it let me cross that item off my bucket list. On one other occasion, I did the same walk but wandered through Brooklyn Heights and was amazed at how beautiful the neighborhood was. I walked by the house used as the exterior for The Cosby Show. Eventually, I made it to a cute walking path near Brooklyn Bridge Park, where I can honestly say that I found what I believe to be the best spot to view the city. Sitting on a bench, looking over at downtown NYC, I was overcome with a sense of awe. Living in such a small town, sometimes it's hard to fathom the scale of something like the Big Apple until you get a chance to see it like this. I have said several times that if I ever moved to NYC, that is probably the neighborhood I would want to live in.

It's also a town that's become a lot more known for film shoots and celebrity spotting. I stood in the crowd while Michael

Emerson (of LOST and Persons of Interest fame) shot a scene in Times Square for Persons of Interest. My wife and I watched James Spader shoot a scene for The Blacklist as our kids played at the beach down near Coney Island. Two friends of mine came with me one year for a weekend trip, and we ended up in the middle of a Conan O'Brien shoot on 6th Ave. When I brought my friend Dale to NYC for the first time, in about two minutes, both Henry Winkler (the Fonz) and Penn Jillette walked by us while we wandered the streets of Times Square.

During one encounter, I was walking back to a subway station after I had bought some theatre tickets. I saw a few people standing on the steps of this building, and one of them caught my attention. He was dressed pretty outrageously, and I remember thinking to myself, "Man, that guy dresses like Pauley Shore." As I walked closer and eventually went by these guys, I looked at the oddly dressed man and suddenly realized that it was, in fact, Pauley Shore sitting on the steps. I smiled and shook my head and kept on rolling.

All things considered, the most memorable "film shoot" experience in NYC for me was in 2017. On a Saturday afternoon, I caught a video on Facebook talking about The Amazing Race. They were kicking off their 30th season from Washington Square Park. I said to my wife, "I wish I was in NYC this weekend," to which she asked me why, and I told her. We are huge fans of the show and would have loved to have been there. She turns to me and says, "Well, we could go." I paused for a few long moments, and she said,

"You're really thinking about going, aren't you?" I was. Within a couple of minutes, I said, "Ok, let's go!" and within the hour, off we went. It had been ages since I had made a trip that spontaneous, and the moment we told the kids, they were jumping for joy.

Fast forward to Sunday afternoon, we arrived at the park in time to see the show getting set up. As massive fans, it was pretty awesome to watch the film crew prep the area. Racers came out to do intros, and the host Phil Keoghan was right there talking to everyone and taking photos while prepping to do his camera work. They had a crane camera set up just in front of us, taking a bunch of shots and other free cameras wandering around getting B-roll footage of the crowd. Assistants were handing out waivers for people to sign if they knew they would end up on camera.

The kids got bored after we were there for several hours, and honestly, who could blame them. My wife and I were the big fans, so my kids didn't quite get why we were sticking around so long. Before we knew it, we could see the field camera and sound people come in, and that was a cue the real action was about to begin. From my own experience with The Amazing Race Canada, I had learned that every team has a camera person and a sound person. So, we knew the teams had to be leaving soon. My wife insisted that as soon as the teams took off, she would try and get a photo with the host Phil.

With a wave of his hand, the race began, and people scattered everywhere. I shot a bunch of footage on my camera of teams running in countless directions before my wife and I met up. She was off to try and find the host but quickly turned back without success. Then as we are standing there talking, Phil walks right by us with his assistant. I pointed to him, and my wife bolted towards him, saying, "Phil! Phil," and as she caught up to him, she told him that we had driven 14 hours to come to see the kickoff and really wanted a photo. He was shocked and said, "14 hours? That's got to be the record. Of course, I can take a picture". He greeted me, and our two kids and his assistant took my wife's phone and said they had enough time for one photo, and that was it. We stood for the pose, thanked him, and then totally freaked out. We really had driven all that way to snap one picture, and at that moment, it was worth all of it.

For my kids, again, they had become quite bored and had wanted to leave more than a few hours ago. But when they saw the look of pure joy on our faces, they too became so happy and excited. After all was said and done, I realized even more so than ever that kids take cues from their parents, and this was a prime example of it. They were bored out of their mind, but the moment they saw how happy we were, they too became delighted. It was a great moment for all of us. The photo of Phil and us comes up on our photo frame in the kitchen now and then, and when it does, the kids always point it out and smile.

There are also moments in a place like New York, where the most random things happen and give you the greatest pleasures. In another book of mine, "The Caravan Chronicles," I wrote about the story of a subway ride where I sang on the car with a random musician. It became one of the biggest highlights of that two-week road trip.

Because NYC is so large and has so much to offer, each time I visit, I have tried to pick out a specific place or thing I want to see during that trip. On one occasion, I found myself having a hard time thinking of where to go. I remembered hearing friends of mine say they wished they could have gone to see "X" or "Y" or something or other. So, I posted a challenge of sorts on Facebook and asked all of my friends to give me a place to visit in NYC, and if they wanted, a specific photo. I got up early on Saturday morning and spent the entire day wandering the city looking for these places. It gave me one of the most unique experiences of NYC. It had me going to locations I had never thought of, which made the whole thing feel so fresh. Paul's Boutique from the Beastie Boys album sent me to a corner in the village, which I had never been to but discovered some pretty wicked little shops in the area. I got challenged to go find Gray's Papaya and have a hotdog. I had seen that place featured on countless shows and movies but had never made my way there. Turns out, the food was pretty gross, but it was yet one more place I could cross off my list. I enjoyed the "tell me where to go" challenge so much I will likely reissue it the next time I visit.

From Coney Island sideshows to countless locations from TV and movies, NYC will always have something new to offer me. It seems that no matter how many times I go there, it never bores me and never lets me down. If you've never had the chance to go, then add it to your to-do list. I hope you can experience all that NYC has to offer.

One Guy in a Car
For
Three Weeks

As I mentioned earlier, in my early 20s, I worked as a pizza delivery driver. As a personal goal, I decided I wanted to reach Los Angeles, Toronto, Vancouver, and New York City, all by the time I was 25. I accomplished that goal before my 24th birthday in 1997 when I took another memorable trip. Each time I had made an extended road trip, I wanted it to be bigger and better than the last one. The year before, I experienced the high of New York City, so now it was time for another goal. I knew that somehow, someway, I would need to get to the other side of the USA and experience Los Angeles and the likes of Hollywood, California.

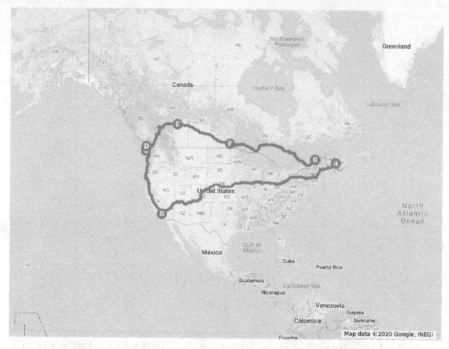

My North American Adventure trip consisted of three weeks of travel and accumulating 15,000 KMs on my car. With only $2,000 to my name, and no one to travel with, I ventured out on my own, and at that time in my life, this was the most ambitious road trip I had ever taken.

While it had been my intention to have a travel companion with me for this trip, as it turned out, he wasn't as committed to saving his money as I was. As the days got closer and closer to the departure date, it became clear this would be a solo trip.

This was the summer of 1997 when gas was cheap, and I'm glad it was because I certainly wasn't driving anything that gave good gas mileage. A blue 1985 Chevrolet Impala was my car of choice. In fact, it was the only car I could use at the time, and if I was going to make the trip, it would have to be in that beast. I had bought a road atlas to use as a guide to get there and back. This was in the days before GPS and Google Maps. On the last page of the atlas, there was a map of North America, and it had distances and driving times between various points. I drew a line from Moncton, NB, to Los Angeles in a straight diagonal line across the United States. I then connected LA to Victoria, BC, and then from there back to Moncton. Knowing that the car could do about 600kms on a tank of gas, I estimated that the total cost of fuel would run me about $1,000. That assumed I was driving 15,000 kilometers. I also knew that I would need money for motels, food, and any novelty items I opted to pick up.

I packed the car up on a Sunday afternoon, and Monday morning at 7am, I began my trek. It was my intention to get from Moncton all the way to Buffalo, NY. Having driven to NYC the year before, I still had a good recollection of the route to take and how far it went. The drive was relatively easy, but not much to see. One of the biggest downfalls of driving through the US is most of the interstate highways have very little to see. Driving through the state of Maine felt like an eternity of trees before I at least started to see something that looked more modern.

If you look it up on Google Maps today, it will tell you that it takes about 14.5 hours to drive from Moncton to Buffalo. In 1997 that was not the case. By the time I got close to Syracuse, which is not that far from Buffalo, I was exhausted. I pulled off the highway into the closest motel I could find and quickly fell asleep. I remember seeing signs for motels and not caring where I would end up as long as I could get a good night's sleep.

Waking up at 6:30am, I took a shower and was on the road again by 7. From Buffalo, I traveled south and drove through Cleveland, Toledo, and eventually made my way to Chicago. Having been to Chicago many times since then, it's still a city I enjoy. Not to the extent of New York mind you, but it's still a great city to visit, and I look forward to every time I get the chance to go back. However, the first time I ever got to see Chicago was one of the most anxiety-ridden experiences of my life.

My original plan was to bypass the city entirely to avoid traffic. When I made my route up, I wasn't all that interested in seeing the city of Chicago and just wanted to maximize my travel time. Like many road trips, things changed along the way. As I had spent so much time driving on endless interstate highways with nothing to see, as I got closer, I changed my mind. It would be nice to actually see something big instead of more trees along the highway. Truth be told, I think I really just wanted to see the Sears Tower (now the Willis Tower) even if it was from my car. If I remember correctly, it was the tallest building in the world at the time. So instead of taking I-80 and heading straight towards Davenport, I took a huge right turn and headed up the I-90 towards the windy city. It was a decision that I wouldn't regret, but at the time, I began to panic.

I was so excited about getting to see the outskirts of Chicago that I didn't bother to pay much attention to the gas gauge in the car.

I had hit the city right around 5:00pm and was in the middle of the supper rush hour. Cars were moving slow, and I finally had the chance to experience what it's like to drive in a bigger city. And it sucked. I remember being excessively impatient and wondering how long it would be before traffic would start moving at a sane pace. The frustration with the traffic would soon give way to a different, more anxious feeling when I spotted the gas gauge leaning heavily to the left. The tank was almost empty.

In what can be best described as an automotive version of claustrophobia, I was becoming quite anxious. With what felt like 1000s of cars around me, and no gas station in sight, the panic began to set in. I turned my music off and sat there and stewed. The car would move a few feet as traffic inched along a bit, and I would look at the gauge again and again. Did the needle move? I think it moved. Is it on the line or just above the line? I wonder how much gas is actually in the tank when the needle is on the line.

The Sears Tower could be seen off to the right as my own anxiety tank was overflowing. Was I going to get to a gas station in time? Eventually, traffic started to speed up, but now the situation was worse because the needle was definitely on the empty line. As the traffic finally started to move, I spotted a sign that said a service station was just a couple of miles ahead. I breathed a huge sigh of relief as I navigated the car across the lanes to get to the exit. As I approached my turn, I spotted what was supposed to be the gas station just beyond the exit. Tore down and under construction, there was no way I was getting fuel there. I pulled back into the main flow of traffic and just kept going hoping that something would come up and save me.

Within ten minutes of that false exit, I spotted another sign for a small community just outside the city. I knew I had to take a chance. I took the exit, and within a minute or two, I found a gas station, filled the tank up, and promised myself I would not let the tank go under half full ever again. To this day, I still fill the tank up on road trips when it dips below half full. On a trip with my friends, we had the gas tank hit quarter full a few times, which made me really nervous. With the tank now full, I continued on my merry way and stopped for the night just outside of Chicago. I don't even remember the name of the place. I just remember that it was night and I was tired, so I stopped driving for that evening.

Already on day three, it was quite lovely to have experienced that much travel in such a short time. However, the hardest part of the trip would come next. See, during those two days, I had driven through several cities, and even though the highways weren't all that interesting, I was never really that bored. I had taken along a little tape recorder to record a journal as I went. Once I left the Chicago area, it was going to be pretty dull until I hit Denver. There weren't any major cities or hell, even towns, on the route I had plotted, and it was a long trip.

What I do remember of that stretch of road was that it was flat farmland all over the place. I kept wondering if this was the area of the country where tornados hit and if I'd end up in the middle of the Twister movie. I also remember that during a stretch through a section of farmland, the clouds did go pretty gray, and the rain was about to come down. As I drove along the road, I spotted a seagull sitting on the highway and hit it dead on. My one and only roadkill on the trip, and in all honesty, it didn't bother me at all. In fact, I remember at the time I was bothered more by the fact that hitting the gull didn't bother me than the fact that I had hit one at all. I think I was so focused on driving through endless fields of grass that I wasn't processing much else.

It was weird when I hit Colorado. I was expecting to see snow or at least mountains, but it was very desert-like. It wasn't until I got right up to Denver itself that I started to see mountains. Once I finally reached the base of the hills, it was an endeavor to get over them. Trying to get that old beast of mine up the mountains was nasty. Those mountains are enormous. Some spots, I couldn't even get the car above 50km/hr because the hills were so steep. I also remember thinking that the Canadian side of the mountains seemed much more beautiful than what I was seeing here. When I finally managed to get through the worst of the hilly parts and to somewhere kind of flat, I found a place to call home for the night.

It was a little ski lodge just outside of Denver. I remember going in and relaxing and calling my dad from the room. My dad lived in Edmonton, and I had told him I was coming through there on my way back and wanted to let him know that all was well. I didn't have that great of a relationship with him but knowing I would get to see him again was comforting.

Initially, I had intended to go from Denver to the Grand Canyon and then stay the night at the canyon and make my way to LA the next day. As things went on, I found out how close I was to Las Vegas. I weighed the idea of going to Vegas or the canyon, and sin city won.

This was Las Vegas in 1997. The Stardust Hotel was still open, and some of the casino experiences people know today weren't around then. Despite all that, I thought the place was amazing. I drove up and down the strip several times just to take pictures. In fact, I stopped at a store and picked up a few rolls of film and burned through all of them, just snapping photos on the strip. I went into the Stardust and gambled a bit just to say that I had. Again, like Chicago, I had no idea I'd be back there repeatedly, so I tried to make the best of it while I was there. Eventually, the fatigue of driving hit me, and I needed to get some sleep. I crashed at a little motel somewhere far from the strip. I woke up to the sound of Howard Stern talking about how relationships were like bowel movements: you can't force them and have to let them happen naturally. This was the first time I had ever heard of Howard Stern. What a sound to wake up to.

Like the other mornings, I got up early and headed out on the road. All things considered, Vegas was not that far from LA, and I knew if I pushed hard, I could be there in no time flat.

With no air conditioning, the drive through the Nevada desert was a hot one. Even with the windows open, there was no cold breeze of any kind to cool me down. The heat was so intense that it's tough to describe. I know that when I had my window down, I put my hand outside to feel the wind rushing against it. I thought this would cool me down a bit, but in fact, the air outside was so hot that it was worse than just being in the car. I had my shorts on and had taken my socks off. It was insanely hot. I made a couple of stops for gas, and I do recall at one point being parked at some service station and noticing that the car was overheating. The vehicle had handled all of the driving thus far quite well, so I let it have a break before pushing on further. Eventually, I made it into the state of California. Before I knew it, LA was coming up on the road signs. I was here. But now what?

Unlike Toronto and New York, I really had no idea what I was going to LA for. I knew that Hollywood was there and that a lot of famous people lived there. Still, beyond that, I knew virtually nothing about the city. I had made no arrangements for accommodations or made any specific plans for what I would do while I was there. I had thought it wouldn't be too hard to find a place to stay, but I also didn't want to pay through the nose for a motel. I also had no maps of the area, and really had no idea where I was going. I finally saw an exit for a street that I had heard of: Santa Monica Blvd. In my head, if Sheryl Crow could write a song about walking along this road, there must be something there. I took the exit and found a convenience store to pick up a couple of maps. From there, I started driving around, trying to look for a place to stay. I managed to find this little hole of a motel near Hollywood Blvd on Vine St, so I paid for my room, unloaded my car, and crashed for a little while.

After getting a little rest, it wasn't long before I wanted to go somewhere. I grabbed my camera and started walking. I knew Hollywood Blvd was close to where I was, so I thought I'd go down there. I walked along the walk of fame and saw a couple of places I had seen on TV. One of them was Mann's Chinese Theater (now known as TCL's Chinese Theatre). This is the place where you see all of the stars put their hand & footprints in the cement. It was pretty cool to be there.

However, shortly after that, I had a bit of a scare. Being a little naive about what life is like in some bigger cities, I walked into a McDonald's and sat down to have my supper. While eating, a man struck up a conversation with me. He saw that I had a camera and started asking me about where I was from and if I had any places I would like to see while I was in town. The conversation seemed harmless at first but eventually led to him wanting me to give him a call later for him to "show me around town." He was an older gentleman, and I had no intention of hanging around LA with some stranger. Needless to say, I grabbed my stuff and headed back to my room a little creeped out. I watched some TV and did my best to put "creepy guy" out of my head, but it would be the first of several things about my trip to LA that didn't go the way I had hoped.

After doing all of this planning for this trip, the one thing I had not planned was what I was going to do once I got to LA. I got there and had virtually no idea what to do. So, the next morning I got up and went back down to the theater and signed up for one of those LA bus tours. It seemed like a good idea, and it made sense since I had no idea where I would end up. The tour ended up being a great idea. The tour bus took me up to see Griffith Park, which gave a great view of the city. It also included the Dorothy Chandler Pavilion, Beverly Hills, and the Hollywood Bowl.

Eventually, I ended up back at the theater with nothing to do, and as it was about 3:30 in the afternoon, I got in my car and went for a drive. I drove all around, just looking at different places, and it was pretty cool. I ended up at the Santa Monica pier. I had gone out there because my friend back home had asked me to bring him back some water from the Pacific Ocean. Santa Monica was a sweet spot to visit, but I didn't stick around there for very long. I ended up just driving around aimlessly for something to do. At one point, I got sort of half lost but made my way back to the motel where I watched some free porn and game shows before I fell asleep.

One good thing did come out of that "creepy guy" at McDonald's. He had suggested that I visit Universal City. He said that it was probably the best place in the city to check out. So, barring any more disturbing incidents, I took his advice and headed over there.

Seeing Universal would prove to be the highlight of my vacation. $37 for admission (now $107) to the park, but that included access to everything there. All of the rides and attractions were part of the admission fee, and it was spectacular. I got to see a lot of cool stuff. The "Back To The Future" ride and attraction was definitely the coolest part. The ride was insane, but I got to see the DeLorean from the movie, plus some behind the scenes special effects used to make the movie. Since then, the Back To The Future stuff has been replaced by newer attractions, but even still, the place is worth seeing.

I got a tour of one of the back lots where they actually shoot movies and saw a lot of different things. From the clock tower in Back To The Future, the famous black van from The A-Team, and even Fred Flintstone's car, all could clearly be seen from the backlot tour. It was truly amazing. I am so glad I went there, and if you ever get the chance to see this place for yourself, don't hesitate.

Now, something you need to know about me is that I'm not the type of tourist who spends hours and hours looking at every tiny little thing in a theme park or museum when I am on my own. I tend to blow through many places trying to see as much as I can in as little time as possible. I've gone through aquariums in an hour and museums in under two. I'm just not the type who typically spends a whole day in one place. So for Universal, I got through it in a few hours and was quite content.

By the time I was done there, I still had lots of energy, and it was only mid-afternoon, so I thought I'd take a trip down to Disneyland. It was never my intention to go on the rides or spend much visiting time there. It was more about going there, snapping some pictures, getting a shirt for someone back home, and leaving. As a dad now, it would be a completely different story if I was to return there, but at the time, it was purely just about something to do.

So, I took some pictures and looked around, but the place was way too crowded. I couldn't believe the number of people there, and it was just unsettling to have that many people in one theme park. I didn't stay long. I paid my admission (which was too much if you didn't go on a ride) and looked around, grabbed some souvenirs, and left.

Now, what I failed to mention to you before was that after I left Universal, I stopped at my motel room briefly. When I got there, I had quite a problem getting the door to close and lock properly. I had to slam it shut repeatedly, and even after that, it would barely lock. I got into a heated argument with the motel manager, which ended in me leaving for Disneyland irritated and a bit fed up with LA.

Looking back at it now, it's clear to me that I spent so much time and effort on planning the actual trip and no planning whatsoever on what I would do once I got there. I've been back to LA several times since then and have had a whole lot more fun and enjoyment while I've been there now. There is plenty to see and do, but you need to be aware of what you want to do and where you want to go. LA is not like NYC in that you can't just go for a walk and find something to do. You need to have transportation and a bit of a plan as to where you want to go. I had the car, but no game plan of any kind. Combine that with meeting "creepy guy" on the first day with a motel room that won't lock and a motel manager who's yelling at you because people are trying to sleep at 1pm in the afternoon. You've got a recipe for an unpleasant experience. When I got back from Disneyland, I demanded a refund for my additional day. I was supposed to stay in LA for four days, so I had pre-paid the motel for that time. With how things had unfolded and how I was feeling at the time, I opted to get one day back and leave on Monday.

I got up Monday morning and headed out. I was now pointed towards Victoria, BC, where my friend Shelly lived. It was at least 18 hours, if not more, from LA, but I was going to make it. Through my travel up the west coast, I drove through San Francisco and across the Golden Gate Bridge. That was definitely the highlight of the trip heading north. Going through downtown SF was neat, too, but crossing the bridge was awesome. I didn't get any decent pictures as it was quite foggy that afternoon, but I've been back to that city since then and have taken a boat tour of the area.

I didn't make it all the way to Victoria without stopping. I paused somewhere along the way and slept for a couple of hours at a rest stop, but it did give me a little bit of sleep that I desperately needed. I remember thinking to myself that I just wanted to get enough sleep to continue on my way and get to Victoria to see Shelly. I really wanted to see someone I knew.

I got to Victoria, and she wasn't home. I had driven all this way, and she was nowhere to be seen. Just as I turned to leave her driveway, I saw a short redhead walking to the house, and that was her. I remember feeling a huge sigh of relief when I saw her as she was the first familiar face I had seen in almost two weeks. She spotted me near her house and came running and gave me a big hug.

My stop in Victoria would prove to have both ups and downs. It was nice to finally see someone I knew and be back in Canada. Shelly and I got in the car, and she gave me the grand tour of the area. She took me up to a beautiful lookout point where we could see most of the city. When we got back to the car, there was smoke coming out of the hood and fluid leaking all the way down the mountain. I managed to get the car down to the bottom and made it to a repair shop. After driving all of this distance, the heater core had died. Thankfully, a visit to Canadian Tire would be the cure for my automobile woes. It also extended my stay by one extra day.

My memories of the extra time in Victoria are pretty foggy, given how long ago it was. I do recall a fascinating visit with one of Shelly's relatives in Qualicum Beach. I can't remember the circumstances as to how we ended up there. But I do clearly remember the very awkward visit I had with her uncle. Shelly had gone inside to talk to her aunt while her uncle and I were outside. He was really into ax throwing and insisted that I give it a shot. I had never met someone so enthusiastic about throwing axes. From the position of my arms to how I released the hatchet, he was meticulous with his directions. It wasn't so much the enthusiasm that caught me off guard, but the fact that ax throwing was even a thing. I'm a city guy through and through, and we were way out in the country, and I started wondering, "Is this what people in the country do for fun?" He insisted I try my hand at it, and as hard as I tried, I never hit anything. This went on for a lot longer than I was ever comfortable with until Shelly finally did come to get me. She asked how things were going, and I could tell by the tone of her voice, she knew that it had been awkward. Otherwise, the visit was quite lovely, and before I knew it, we were heading back to Victoria for the night.

I left Victoria with the intention of staying in Vancouver a day, but that didn't happen. Vancouver was the last city I had wanted to see on my trip. With the limited amount of time I had left, I opted to just drive through the city. Although I didn't do any sightseeing while I was there, I was happy to cross that city off my list. Eventually, I would get a chance to see Vancouver in more detail. Still, for now, I opted to push towards my dad's place in Edmonton and see how close I could get in the next day or so.

I kept on trucking through to Alberta and eventually hit Jasper and the Rocky Mountains. Yes, as I thought, they looked much more beautiful on the Canadian side as they have more snow on the top. I also think they looked nicer because they were in my home province of Alberta. As I passed through Jasper, I had a minor delay as I had to wait for two bear cubs and their mother to get out of the way and cross the road. I wasn't messing with any bears. I managed to get all the way to a place called Hinton. I met up with an old high school friend and crashed at his home for the night.

Now, remember that this was 1997, and the internet was still pretty young at that point. Even still, I was a guy who spent a lot of time online, and up until then, I had not had any internet access for my entire trip. These were the days with no internet-connected phones or tablets. Laptops were luxury items that no pizza delivery guy like me was ever going to be able to afford. So, once I got to my friend's house, I went online and caught up with the latest things back home, and the next day I headed out.

Since my dad lived in Edmonton, I had chosen to stop there during my trip back home. I took the 3-hour drive up to Edmonton and stayed the weekend. The chance to visit with him made a pleasant two-day pitstop before heading home. It was a much more emotional departure for me than it had been before. To make a long story short, every time I went to visit him, I always assumed it would be the last time I would see him. I remember crying in the car as I drove out of his parking lot and wondered if I would ever see him alive again. As it turned out, I did. I got a few more visits before he passed away in 2010.

As I left Edmonton, I made the conscious decision that I was going to get home as soon as possible and went from Edmonton to Winnipeg non-stop. When you hear the stories about the prairies in Canada being flat and dull, they are all true. Nothing but wheat fields and farms for miles and miles are all you see. Even the road itself was boring as it was one long continuous straight line that seemed to go on forever. I got my very first, and only so far, speeding ticket along that stretch when I tried to pass a bunch of cars and got caught by a fancy highway police vehicle.

I got through the city of Winnipeg and was on the east side when I spotted a campground. I figured it would make a comfortable place to stop for the night. I pulled into a campsite, turned the car off, and slept for a few hours and was gone before the site opened up in the morning. I then drove straight through to around Wawa,

Ontario, where I got a little cabin and ate and slept. The only thing I remember about that leg of the trip was that I thought I had seen a dead body on the side of the road. It was late at night, and I didn't know the area at all, so I just kept on trucking through.

From there, I drove straight past Quebec City, where I slept for about 3 hours in a rest stop and then continued all the way back to Moncton. I remember stopping at a McDonald's somewhere along the route and it being in the middle of the night, and they didn't have breakfast at that time. I was so anxious to get back home and into my own bed that nothing was going to slow me down now.

After what felt like an eternity, I finally started to spot the exits for Moncton and opted to go straight to work. No, I wasn't working that day, but I did have a paycheque to pick up. I popped into the store, grabbed my cheque, and realized despite having been up all night, I was actually wide awake. I opted to go over to the other side of town and visit a friend of mine at her work. We chatted for a while, and then eventually, I went home, slept, and let the entirety of the trip finally sink in.

That particular trip proved a few things to me. For starters, it proved that you really do need to have at least some kind of plan about what you're going to do when you go somewhere. Just showing up and figuring it out when you get there is not a great idea. Even if it's not a full itinerary of things to do, at least have a few ideas in mind.

It also proved that when they say life is a journey, not a

destination, it's absolutely right. That trip was proof that the actual target was not the most memorable of things on that trip. It was the trip itself. Driving and driving for miles and miles with no one to talk to. Recording myself on a tape recorder just to keep me company and from being bored was about the only way I stayed sane. I've listened to those tapes a few times, and there are entire sections where I just babble on and on for no reason.

When all was said and done, I could pat myself on the back that I accomplished an amazing trip like this. I put my mind to a task and never lost focus of it and made it a reality. I also was conscious of the fact that if I didn't do it then, I might never get to do that kind of thing again in my life. That fall, I went back to college and did my final speech for "public speaking" class about my trip and how I did it because I didn't know if I would ever get the chance again. I got engaged that same year while in college and married a year later. I then moved to the US for a job, and then "grown-up life" took over from there. It would be a good 10 years after that before I would realize again that you need to seize the moment and take the opportunities when they are there. It's a lesson I taught myself in 1997, and then re-learned again almost 15 years later.

The Road Less Traveled

When it comes to travel, most people head somewhere either because they have to or they want to. Usually, when you "have to" go somewhere, it's because of an obligation you are committed to, such as work or personal engagement. When you "want to" travel to a destination, it's usually for pleasure, such as a vacation or some other getaway. Whether you are obligated to go or want to go, sometimes the destination represents something much more extensive than what appears on the surface. This chapter takes you on a journey through two places that may not have much meaning to you. But for me, these places have been transformative. The story of revisiting my own past through these cities helped forge my path to a much happier future.

Since 1985, I have been proud to refer to Moncton, New Brunswick, as my home, but my life didn't start here. I was born in Edmonton, Alberta, and lived there for almost 12 years. I moved from Edmonton to Moncton in the summer of 1985. My mom opted to move back to her hometown after my father and her split up.

In 1994, I had been living in Moncton for nine years. I had not seen my father in all of that time. Neither he nor my mother had the financial means for either of us to visit. In April of that year, I got a bit of a windfall from a programming job, so I opted to fly out to see him. I had hoped to spend time back in Edmonton to reacquaint myself with where I had been born and a dad I barely knew.

When I left Edmonton, I was 11 years old, and when I returned, I was 20. So, in a way, you could say that I left Edmonton as a child and returned as a man. The visions and memories I had of those years in Edmonton were still prevalent but were those of a kid. When I arrived at the Edmonton airport in April of 1994, I was excited to see my dad but only had faint memories of him from when I was a child. When I walked into the waiting area, a man approached me wearing a tan suede jacket and greeted me. It was my dad, and I didn't recognize him at all until he spoke. He took my suitcase, and we chatted while he drove us back to his home.

I had planned to spend three weeks in Edmonton as I bought an open-ended plane ticket. After one week around my dad, I found myself wanting to come home early. I called home to talk to my mom and broke down. I sobbed as I told her that this was not the man I remembered at all. He was different somehow, and in some ways, it felt like he had given up on the world. He spoke of using weird spells and things to summon spirits into his home, of bizarre conspiracies with the government, and his dissatisfaction with how the city and province were being run. This was not the man I remembered from my childhood.

The call home settled my nerves, and I lasted one more week before deciding to come back home to Moncton. I think the cry on the phone got the worst things out of me as I recall the second week of that trip to be far more positive than the first. By the time the second week was up, I was ready to come home.

In 1997, and then in 2003, I also had the opportunity to revisit Edmonton and my father. Those visits were much more positive than my original as it seemed the shock and awe of what my dad had become had worn off. I was in a better place to simply accept him as the person he was and not the person I remembered. Those visits went surprisingly well and allowed me to visit many places I had experienced as a kid but from the eyes of an adult. A lot of reminiscing went on as I looked at places I lived, the schools I attended, the parks I played in.

Between then and 2015, I visited Edmonton and my family a couple more times. My wife accompanied me on one visit when we told my dad we were expecting our first child. However, it was the last visit in 2015 that was far more emotional than anything I could have ever expected. In 2010, my dad passed away, and at that moment, I suspected I would never return to Edmonton as it was always a place I went only to visit him. But in 2015, I got a work assignment to teach a class in Edmonton, so off I went. I knew it would be weird, but I had no idea how strange and emotional it was actually going to be.

This was the first time I would visit this place without my dad being there. Every time I had come back, I always had my dad to go back to. It was somehow bound to my past and part of my life there. Now with him gone, it seemed that connection was gone as well. I do have a few relatives there (uncles, aunts, even a half-sister). Still, my most significant relationship to that place had always been my father.

Upon arrival, the first thing I did was visit the places I used to live and hang out in. I even went by my dad's old home, knowing he wasn't there, but I somehow felt compelled to drive by. It was kind of neat to see these places again, but nothing really jumped out at me. That is until my last day there.

I had a flight to catch on Saturday evening, so I got up early that morning and decided to go to a park near where I used to live. I spent a little time in there then decided I really wanted to go back to the neighborhood I lived in and re-trace my steps as a child walking to school. I have no idea why I felt compelled to do this. Still, over the few days I was in Edmonton, it kept feeling more and more like this was likely to be my last time there, and if I ever wanted to do anything, now was the time.

My most prominent memories of that city were while I lived at 389 Hooper Crescent, the home I lived in from grades 3-6. I parked the car in front of some houses and went for a walk. I stood in the parking lot and stared around and just soaked it in. My mind was flooded with images from years gone by. I remembered playing street hockey from one end of the parking lot to another. I could almost taste the freezies from the ice cream bike that would come through there. Thousands of images and memories, meaningless to anyone else, but have stuck with me through all these years flashed before me. I then stood about ten feet or so from the door of the place I used to live. The black mailbox with 389 on it just stared at me. Again, more images of the past flooding to the forefront. From ghosts in my kitchen to watching the hockey game in the dark, I felt like a ten-year-old again. The home I lived in was part of a townhouse complex, so there were "blocks" of homes attached together as one building and several buildings altogether in that area.

I walked between two of the townhouses and down the path I used to take to school every day. I went up the hill and into the middle of a big field just beside the old school. The entire time I walked, I had so many childhood memories coming back to me. I stood in the middle of this big field of green grass and remembered watching kids play ice hockey in a homemade rink in the area. I remembered my mom and me setting off model rockets and wondering where they were going to land. I remembered walking through what felt like mountains of snow trying to get to school, as it seemed like they never canceled classes in those days. As I took a few more steps towards my old school and stood at the top of this hill, the tears started to come.

I stood there, with no one around to see how ridiculous I looked, and I bawled hysterically. Not misty-eyed like you get from a sappy movie or a feel-good song. I'm talking hysterical sobbing. I cried and cried for a few minutes and had no idea where it was all coming from. I'm not a man who cries very often, and I couldn't recall any other time in my life that I have wept that hard, but it just kept coming and coming like a dam that had just blown. I let it all out as I looked around until it just seemed to ease off. I shook my head and turned around and looked at the school. I walked over to the yellow doors and stared at the brick wall and remembered so many days of losing so many hockey cards to some stupid game where we threw them against the wall. I remembered us kids using the plastic tags off bread bags and flicking them at each other to the point that the principal made a school announcement banning the game.

I walked around front, took a few pictures, smiled a bit as I peeked inside, then went back to the rear of the building, and just stared for a minute. At that moment, I realized that it had been 30 years since I left Edmonton. And at that moment, I also remembered the face of the last person I ever saw at the school: Mr. Schlotter.

He was my all-time favorite schoolteacher and someone I will never, ever forget. I remembered him and I talking about some computer things I wanted and then saying goodbye. I also remembered that in 2003 I had visited my dad and came to the school hoping Mr. Schlotter would be there, and sure enough, he was. I smiled as I remembered that as a kid, he was taller than me, but as an adult, I was taller than him. I remembered telling him he was a great teacher and him telling me he was glad to see I had turned out well. We shook hands, and I said goodbye. Today, standing there behind the school, I got misty-eyed this time, and with no one around, I smiled at the school and said, "Goodbye, Mr. Schlotter."

I walked back to my car, started it up, and drove away. At that moment, it felt like I would not be returning to Edmonton again.

I repeated this same kind of experience when I went to my other neighborhood. I walked the old way to my other old school, wandered around, and had plenty of memory flashes, but this time it wasn't as emotional. I think whatever I was feeling came out in that field near Overlander's School, and I was genuinely ready to go.

I visited a couple of other places I knew as a kid, then headed to the airport and couldn't wait to get out of there. Driving towards the airport, I did not expect to ever return to that city. I think that's why standing in that field was so emotional.

I knew it was going to be weird, not seeing my dad. What I didn't expect was to have so much emotion bubble to the surface when seeing these places. They are a part of me that had been almost forgotten. When you don't think about something, it's not that it's forgotten. It just gets buried behind everything else.

I've had so much happen to me in that 30-year time period that most of what I experienced in Edmonton is not something I think about or really talk about anymore. As I push towards 50, there's more of my past where I am now, than there was in Edmonton.

Even though I had returned multiple times since I moved, this one was very different because it really did have a sense of finality. It was almost like saying goodbye to my dad again and closing the door on that chapter of my life.

As for what went on when I was standing in the field and how I felt, I think it was a catharsis of sorts that was long overdue. When I moved from Edmonton to Moncton in 1985, it was really hard. Junior high at Queen E was pure hell as I endured the worst bullying of my entire life during that time. The trying times in school over those three years was only made tolerable by making a handful of friends and falling in love for the first time. A beautiful strawberry blonde girl that I had become so enamored with somehow made school tolerable.

We all feel a pull towards things in our past. So when we visit a place that represents something from our own personal history, it's going to bring up emotions of all sorts. I think at that moment on the hill, the ramifications of how my life unfolded as a result of moving away became clear. I think all of my pre-teen anger came out in those tears. It was an incredibly cathartic experience, which gave me a very different view of Edmonton than I had before that final trip.

The places that we are connected to via personal history and experiences will always bring back many memories when you revisit them. And even in cases where those memories are not good ones, I have found it can be healthy to force yourself to experience them. Edmonton was my prime example of this, but I also experienced a similar, albeit on a smaller scale, feeling when I revisited Poughkeepsie for the first time. The second city from my past that helped me move forward.

Poughkeepsie (puh-kip-see) was the place I lived in upstate New York for a year. Although I only lived there for a short period, my first time revisiting that city evoked similar emotions to those I experienced in Edmonton. During a work trip, I took my rental car for a drive up to that area. I drove by the old IBM campus I worked at, my old apartment, and many of the places I was familiar with from the city. It brought back a surplus of memories of my time there. It also forced me to deal with some of my demons from that period of my life.

For many years I found myself regretting the decision to move back to Moncton while I was down there. I had a huge opportunity to remain at IBM and grow a successful career there. Still, I opted for personal reasons to return home. That regret stayed with me for ages as it took me a long time to get my career back to a place I was content with. Driving into the parking lot of my old apartment, it hit me again. I had another emotional reaction to being in a place from my past.

I found the regret I experienced for so many years was gone. I realized in those moments that my life had taken a path that it needed to. It led me to where I was now, and although at the time I was angry and sad about the loss of a job, it brought me to the best job and career I could have ever hoped for. Moving back to Moncton also resulted in the collapse of my first marriage, which sent me over the edge and into the hospital after a failed suicide attempt. I came out of that experience and realized that something in my life had to change. I got together with the woman who would become my wife the following year and married her two years later. My life has changed so dramatically because of the lessons I have learned. Taking a trip into the past is part of what has allowed me to grow.

In the parking lot of my old apartment building in Poughkeepsie, I turned my back on my negative thoughts of that era for good and have never had regret since. I don't believe in regrets and now see that even mistakes can be opportunities to learn to change and improve oneself. It may sound a bit new age or psycho-babble-ish, but the proof is in the pudding. I wouldn't be where I am now without having experienced the things I have gone through.

Traveling to exciting locations and cities is great for both pleasure and work. Still, there is definitely merit in visiting places that might seem a bit more mundane to others but have significant meaning to you personally. Sometimes a trip to the past is as helpful as one to a beach or resort. Don't be afraid to connect with parts of your life again. It may help you find clarity.

Angels and Revelations

After visiting LA for a brief few days in 1997, I wasn't in a rush to return. My first visit to the city had left a bad taste in my mouth, and I was pretty content to never return. As time passed, though, and new and more exciting opportunities presented themselves, I found myself back there. Upon my return, the city that I came back to was not the city that I had remembered visiting. It had been 13 years, and many things had changed, including me. Subsequent visits to LA would be filled with plenty of other noteworthy experiences. However, that first return set the stage for more memorable days to come.

In 2010, I chose to take a quick trip to LA with my friend Billy to catch a reunion concert of my all-time favorite band, Faith No More. I could write several chapters about how that band has influenced me over the years. They broke up in 1998, and this show in LA was supposed to be their last reunion gig in North America. It wasn't, but at the time, I knew I wanted to see them play again, so I used all of my frequent flyer and hotel points to book myself and my friend a flight to LA, and we spent two nights there.

The first thing that was different about LA was this time, I was going with a particular purpose. I knew that the typical tourist stuff would pop up and be part of the trip, but the focus was on something both me and my friend were really looking forward to. Further to that, taking an old friend like Billy with me made a huge difference. He'd been a few places here and there, but LA was new for him. Much like some of my other excursions, this trip was also about sharing the experience with someone else. I also have to admit that being able to fly across the country and get to LA in a single day versus 5 days also helped as I wasn't exhausted by the time we got there.

We upgraded my rental car to a fancy sports car and made a quick stop at the famous Randy's Donuts, followed by driving around the city for an hour or so. We eventually made our way to the hotel, which was right on Hollywood Blvd. If you've never been to

LA, the one thing you may not realize about Hollywood Blvd and the walk of fame is that it's not a great place to be. In 1997, the area was covered with homeless people, bums, and many seedy shops. This time, the neighborhood was in far better shape than it had been, but still had some room for improvement. It didn't matter because the concert was literally across the street from the hotel we were at.

In making my travel arrangements, I wanted to try and stay at a hotel that was a bit more high end. Somewhere that was somewhat reputable and would not be anything like the last place I stayed at when I was there. As a frequent traveler, I had accumulated a lot of points. Between the points and some cash, I got a really nice room at the W Hollywood Hotel. Rooms ran about $400/night for a closet, so using my points definitely helped saved some coin. I assumed it was meant to be high end but didn't realize how nice it was until we walked into it.

We got up to our room, and although it was a regular-sized room, it was better than most places I had stayed in before. With a marble shower with glass doors, two huge beds, 42" LCD flat-screen TV, and all the bells and whistles you needed, we were living in style. One of the more obscure means you can tell the scale of a hotel is by the room service menu, and by how much stuff in the mini-bar costs you—one bottle of water: $9. One can of Pepsi: $5. A steak: $38. On top of all that, they had a menu specific for pets. Yes, pets. We were in LA, seeing our favorite band, driving a fancy sports car, and staying at an expensive hotel. You couldn't really get much more Hollywood than that. However, the room had nothing on what would happen next.

After unpacking and putting our feet up for a while, we decided to head out and get some food. We walked out the front of the hotel onto Hollywood Blvd and were not sure where to go. We had already been down one part of it, but we decided to go back to that same area and see what we could find for food.

Walking along the boulevard, we were sort of half stopped beside this restaurant named Juicy Burger as we pondered where to go. As Billy & I both looked into the window of the restaurant, we noticed a man with long grey dreadlocks. Double take: it was Mike "Puffy" Bordin from Faith No More sitting there with Jon Hudson, the guitar player from Faith No More, having supper. Billy and I very quickly decided that we were going to have our meal at the Juicy Burger.

We ordered our food and sat down literally at the same "bar" where the FNM guys were. We ate our food and deliberated on how to break the ice or what to say to them. As Puffy went to go for his coat, my friend spoke up and introduced himself. We then had a 10-minute conversation with Puffy and Jon talking about shows, how far we had come, having seen them before, and a ton of stuff. Puffy told us to expect to hear some old songs at the show tomorrow night. They posed for a few pictures, said thanks for coming out, shook our hands, and were on their way.

When I think about "being in the right place at the right time," this is one of those moments. I mentioned in a previous chapter about getting the photo with Phil Keoghan from The Amazing Race. This happenstance run-in with two guys from Faith No More felt very serendipitous. It made the show and the entire trip far more memorable than I could have asked for.

The next night, Billy and I walked across the street and got in line for the concert. We both stood there in t-shirts and shorts while everyone else had jackets and even hoodies on. In talking with others waiting in line with us, we mentioned we were from Canada. People then began to chuckle as they realized why we were the only ones dressed in summer clothes. The "cold" weather in late November wasn't a problem for us. The show started off slow with some not so great acts, but once the band hit the stage, it was a few hours of pure glee. Billy and I cheered on and sang along with countless tunes and just soaked up every minute we could of seeing this incredible act. The show ended, we crashed at the hotel, got up the next morning, and came home. It was a fantastic journey that allowed me to look at LA with a different perspective.

Once I put that trip behind me, my thoughts about LA changed considerably. I found myself wanting to return from time to time. I've always had a fascination with how television and movies are filmed. Visiting LA now and then has given me a bit more of a window into what that world looks like.

I had the chance to attend an LA Live Talks show that featured Felicia Day and Wil Wheaton. A friend of mine turned me on to Felicia's work in The Guild. Then not long later, I recognized her when she joined the cast of Eureka for part of season four and five. I knew of Wil Wheaton from "Star Trek: The Next Generation" and his role in "Stand By Me." Wil would be interviewing Felicia about her book with a signing afterward. I had read her book and learned that she was a huge Anne of Green Gables fan. Living in New Brunswick, PEI is only an hour or so away, so I went over to the island and picked up some swag and brought it to the show. When she signed my book, I told her where I was from and that I had real PEI swag for her. She got pretty excited and then posed for a photo with one of the items I had brought for her.

At the end of the night, I was outside wondering if Wil Wheaton was going to come out, and sure enough, he did. He didn't chat for long, but he did stay long enough to sign my Stand By Me movie. As I am a huge science fiction fan, it may come as a surprise to many people that Stand By Me is, hands down, my all-time favorite movie. The story is about four young boys who go off in search of the dead body of one of their classmates who had gone missing. As a teenager and young adult, I had three very close friends, I hung out with almost every day. When I watch that movie, it's almost like watching a piece of my own history on film.

In the spring of 2007, one of those close friends of mine passed away unexpectedly. Shortly after, I sat down and re-watched Stand By Me. As Gordy tells the story about the fate of his good friend Chris, the tears started to come. All I could do was think about my old friend and how I'd never see him again. It's for this reason, I still feel such a connection to that movie.

For me, my late good friend J.C. collapsed in a bar and was taken to a hospital where he later died. Watching that story unfold onscreen was like saying goodbye to my long-time friend whom I would never get to see again. So even though it is just a movie, and I know Wil Wheaton was playing a character, the opportunity to meet him was a real honor for me.

If you are a fan of movies and television, there are plenty of places you can visit in LA that have been used for filming. One for me was Vasquez Rocks. You've probably never heard of it by name, but you've definitely seen them before. Vasquez Rocks are a very well known desert mountain area just outside of LA where a lot of exterior filming is done. The original Star Trek shot a lot of episodes out there. I had seen the desert area countless times on movies and TV but only heard the actual name through The Big Bang Theory. I went up for a drive, and sure enough, they were wrapping a shoot for something when I got there. I climbed one of the rocks I had seen a dozen times on TV and felt pretty cool to be part of such a landmark of television and film history. In fact, I recorded a bunch of videos of me in that area and posted it to YouTube using some cheesy Star Trek fight music to add some flare. All of that would pale compared to my most significant experience with television in Los Angeles in 2016.

On February 26th, 2016, I did the Warner Brothers studio tour. This tour takes you through the entire backlot, where you get to see where a lot of popular television programs were shot. I sat on the actual Central Perk couch from Friends. I stood in the classroom from Pretty Little Liars. I even got to stand in the bleachers from the set of The Big Bang Theory. As a huge TV buff, I was pretty much in heaven seeing all of these fantastic places that were part of TV and movie history. The visit to the Warner Brothers lot was actually the warm-up gig for my next and most memorable moment in Los Angeles.

When I first started traveling for work, I spent a lot of time in my evenings trying to see and explore the area as much as I could. I mean, someone else was paying me to be in a foreign city, so I might as well make the best of it. As time wore on, I found myself more and more tired at the end of a day and would end up sitting in my hotel room, watching TV and going to bed, or opting to skip the TV and start writing chapters like this one. Every now and then, I'd make plans to do something while I was there. Those were usually the more memorable trips. This one particular visit to LA was the personification of cool things to do for fans of TV. I went to see a taping of The Big Bang Theory.

If you do enough Googling, you'll come to learn that getting tickets to a TV show is actually free. There's no charge to see a TV show taping, but getting a guaranteed ticket can be challenging. The Big Bang Theory was television's highest-rated comedy at the time, so tickets would go fast on their website when they became available. I secured a single standby ticket, which didn't guarantee me a seat. It did however allow me a chance to acquire a seat if one was available on taping day. After doing a ton of research on how standby tickets work, I formulated a plan. I'd show up really early, and hopefully, be the first in line for standby and then have the best chance at getting a seat.

Since the show taped on Tuesday, I spent the better part of Monday researching everything I needed to know for tape day. From where to park, when to be there, and how the lines worked, I was ready to go. The night before the taping, I was so anxious that I had a hard time sleeping. I ended up awake around 5am so I got up, had a shower, and left.

Both Big Bang and Ellen share the same waiting area, but Ellen tapes at 5:00pm and Big Bang at 6:30pm. That meant that the Big Bang folks can't use the line inside until after Ellen's audience has been seated. As a result, a self-policing line forms in the parking lot. When the Ellen group leaves, they move the Big Bang folks from outside to inside.

I got there, parked my car, and walked over to the empty lot to find not a soul there. I was indeed person #1. The time was 5:48am. I then went inside to the visitor's center and asked them where to wait, and they confirmed it was outside.

I didn't see another soul in that parking lot until around 8:30 when another standby ticket holder came in. She had been coming to the tapings since season 4. She'd met the cast, crew, been on the actual set, and knew a lot about how the whole thing worked. She assured me that it was pretty good odds we would be getting in. The day didn't seem to drag on at all until we got moved inside. Once we were brought into the parking garage, around 4pm, the waiting became unbearable. It would be at least another hour and a half before I would know if I was going into the taping. I had been there for 10+ hours, but the last 90 minutes was a killer. I was never so anxious about seeing a show as I was at this point.

Security eventually checked my ID and stamped my hand, and I waited some more. VIPs started going in and then guaranteed folks next. The secured line emptied, and more VIPs went in. I was getting even more anxious and doing my best to try and stay positive. Then out of nowhere, one of the pages called out, "Standby numbers 1-10, let's go". The first 10 in the line were going to be admitted. My heart was pounding with excitement, and I couldn't believe it was actually going to happen. We were led across the street and entered the studio lot. I kid you not in saying that I was almost in tears as I crossed the road as I could not believe this was actually happening.

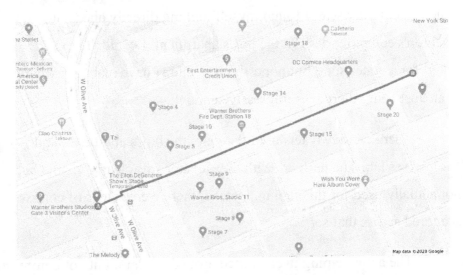

I have been very fortunate and lucky to experience many

things in my life. Still, every once in a while, I hear a voice in my head saying, "Is this really happening? Am I really going to do this?" Walking across that street and going into the studio lot to see the taping was one of those moments. Overcome with emotion and just utterly astounded by the idea that this was actually happening, it would have been easy to burst into tears in excitement.

Our group went through several security points, had our bags checked twice, told to use the bathroom, and eventually led us down to Stage 25, which is the stage the show is taped on. Once inside, all our bags were searched again. Cell phones were tagged and kept until the end of the taping. I followed around a corner and up a set of stairs where I was about to be seated. Peggy (whom I had met in line), knowing the people there, quietly asked for a seat on the right side of the stage. Apparently, it's a big no-no to ask, and she was even told that she's not really supposed to do that, but it was okay. When I got to my seat, I found myself looking directly ahead at Sheldon's computer desk in the boy's apartment. I couldn't have asked for a better spot, but honestly, it wouldn't have mattered where I sat. Just being there was impressive enough.

There were two sets used that day: the boy's apartment and Wolowitz's lab. The hallway with the elevator was clearly visible but not actually used for this taping. Instead, there were stacks of chairs scattered across that set.

The actual taping itself started around 6:30pm, but not before we all got a little treat. The producers ran the episode "The

Application Deterioration" (9×18) on the monitors for everyone to watch. This had been taped the week before and had not aired yet. Once the episode was over, the actual taping began. Episode 9×19 – The Solder Diversion Excursion was my episode.

Before anything was shot or shown to us, they introduced the cast to the audience one at a time, and they all came out to wave to us. Once that was done, the episode began.

Watching the taping itself was absolutely amazing. As someone who was a massive fan of the show, getting to be there and see them put it all together was incredible. I had seen David Letterman before, but this was something different.

They would call cut, then do a scene again with slightly different lines. If you watched closely enough, you'd pick up on little things the actors were doing that you wouldn't notice otherwise. Jim Parsons puts his script notes on small recipe cards and studies them between takes. Just before they shoot, he put them in a drawer in the kitchen of the apartment.

Between takes, you would see the cast goofing off with each other, or pacing around and waiting. Johnny Galecki studied his lines a bit, and I spotted Kaley playing on her phone quite a bit. Both Johnny and Melissa Rauch took their glasses off when they were not on camera. When they called to start, everyone got into their positions, and away they went.

Eventually, we did get a few little "bloopers" from both

Kaley and Melissa. Nothing too crazy, but they forgot a line or messed up one here and there, but for the most part, these people were nailing it. You can tell they do this for a living.

To get a feel for what it actually is like, imagine you are in front of Sheldon's desk looking straight at it. Then take about 15 steps backward and raise yourself in the air about 15-20 feet or so. That was where I was. The lab set, which was to the right of the apartment, was literally on the other side of the wall. The window in the kitchen of the boy's apartment literally goes nowhere, and the lab is right on the other side. On the far right side of the lab set, there is a door that the girls come in through. That door literally leads to an empty hallway on the stage which leads to the audience if you turn right.

For a couple of the scenes that I saw, they were pre-taped the day before, but the cast re-did them for the audience. A scene with Sheldon and Amy in her car was re-enacted with them sitting on two chairs on the hallway set.

While they were re-writing one of the lines from the lab scenes, Johnny grabbed a bunch of what looked like dryer tubing and pointed it to Kaley's ear. She had her back turned to him, so she didn't know he was there. He must have said "boo" or something because she yelped quite loudly, and the audience heard her and started laughing. The two of them laughed and kept on trucking.

Shortly before the taping was over and between takes, the host introduced Johnny & Kaley to the audience. Both came up and stood on the rail and thanked the crowd. They were very gracious and excited to be there and told us that as long as we kept watching, they would keep making new episodes. The did manage to go three more seasons.

They filmed the last scene, called cut, and that was it. Everyone piled out of there and out of the studio some quickly. I got back to the car within about 10 minutes, posted a photo of my program from the show on Instagram, and that was it. No, I didn't get to meet any of the cast, but I didn't care. The entire experience was incredible, but it was what came after the taping that really hit home.

Most times, I tend to think of myself as being kind of humble. I don't like to brag about the things I have done, but I do love to share my experiences with people. When I posted the photo of my Big Bang program to Facebook, I got a ton of comments, one of which was from my friend Katie. I don't imagine her comment was anything that would stand out to her, but it's one that I took to heart and, in its own way, resulted in the very book you are reading.

Katie Lynn In all seriousness, you need to write a memoir. I'd help edit. Seriously, you do the coolest stuff.

Sure, we all feel pretty good about ourselves when we get to do something pretty cool. And when you post it to Facebook and a bunch of your friends comment in on what you did, it gives you a tiny ego boost. You feel like, "Hey, maybe I am kind of cool," even if it is just for a moment.

When I saw her comment, it really made me think about how

lucky I have been. Having the opportunity to travel the world has opened my eyes to so many new experiences. It's like living in the same house for years, only to discover there's an entire floor you never knew existed. I managed to get a good job, the best wife, great kids, awesome friends and family, and then I get to throw in these memorable experiences on top of that. It made me feel truly blessed.

And with a chance of sounding a bit full of myself, I also realized that there are many people I know that will never get to do or see a fraction of the things that I get to do. So they live vicariously through my own adventures. I've had countless people tell me to keep posting my travel stories on Facebook because they love to hear about what kind of new experiences I've had.

This led me to another realization about those same people. Similarly, I look up to others and wish I could be doing the things they do, some people are looking at me and thinking the same thing about me, and I'm nobody. I'm just a geek from Riverview who got lucky enough to somehow end up in all of these different places, experiencing unique things. I came to understand at a much deeper level how much I need to truly appreciate what I have, and not focus so much on the negative.

I've spent a good part of my life tending to emphasize on what I don't have, or the negative side of pretty much anything. I have struggled considerably to try to turn my opinion towards the positive because I know it's healthier for me, making me a happier person. In seeing Katie's comment on Facebook, it put a big smile on my face. It made me realize that I do have a lot to be thankful for, and I have no reason to spend so much time focused on the negative.

It wasn't long after that comment on Facebook that I started compiling all these travel stories that would eventually make up this book. In a way, I have The Big Bang Theory and my friend Katie to thank for inspiring me to create something of my own that I could share with others. I've been writing in one form or another for as long as I can remember. This, however, is the first time I have written something to this extent. I'm curious to see where it will lead me. For all I know, this book will be my own "big bang" that leads to even bigger experiences in my life. But I digress.

For LA, from book signings to TV show tapings, Los Angeles has been a city that I now enjoy returning to. It has a very different type of personality compared to other cities. Los Angeles is also not a city you want to be visiting without a car, so be sure to have some kind of wheels to get you around. Most of all, enjoy yourself. Whether it's peeking behind the curtain of television and movies, or visiting a beach and soaking up the sun, there are plenty of things one can do there to revel in.

The Perils of Frequent Travel

As someone who has become a seasoned traveler, I share a common trait with other road warriors out there. We don't have much patience for those who only travel from time to time. This is the story of why frequent travelers love to travel but hate the mechanics of travel.

Just recently, I was on a flight from London, England, back to Toronto. Having status with the airline, I can board the aircraft before most regular passengers, which is a pretty common perk of someone who travels enough for business. The next time you get on a plane and see people scattered throughout the cabin, take a closer look. You're likely to notice that many of those "pre-board" folks are business passengers.

I sat down in my seat and heard someone say something about flying for business. I made the comment that the "novelty" of flying is quite common for those on vacation. Still, for business travelers, the excitement of getting on a plane ended after the third or fourth business trip. A young man sitting in front of me turned and said, "It ends after the first trip." I smiled, unpacked my tablet and headphones, sat in my seat, and disappeared into a movie while the rest of the plane boarded.

To best describe how it truly is different, let's look at the average person who might take a vacation once every now and then. This person, let's call him Mike, goes to Florida, or somewhere tropical with his wife. Or maybe he takes a trip to Vegas for a bachelor party. In Mike's world, travel is not something he does very often.

Mike gets to the airport late because he doesn't know when he's supposed to get there. He didn't check-in online, so he's waiting in the check-in area and finally gets his bag checked and his boarding passes. Mike makes his way to security, and when he finally gets to the screening, he doesn't have his boarding pass with him because he put it in his bag. He doesn't know to hold onto it until he gets screened. He also forgets to take his laptop out of his carry-on and remove any liquids he has. For that matter, he brought along his cologne, which is too big, and he gets mad about security throwing it out. He goes through the metal detector but didn't take his belt off, so the machine beeps, and he has to go through a second time.

He finally gets to his gate and waits for them to call boarding. He hears something about his flight beginning to board, and he sees a line form, so he gets in line. When he gets to the agent, he's told that he can't board because they aren't boarding his zone yet. He gets out of line and waits for his zone to be called and eventually makes his way onto the plane.

When Mike finally gets onto the plane, he's asked for his boarding pass again, and since he put it in his jacket, he's now digging for it while a line forms behind him. He then gets confused by where his seat is and eventually does find it but decides he really needs to fold his jacket up and put it in the overhead space. Mike then can't find room for his bag because it's too large to be on this aircraft or he was in the last zone, and all the overhead space is taken up. He finally gets his bag sorted, sits down, and finally, people start finishing the boarding process. He then realizes he needs something out of his bag. Since he had the window seat and someone else has sat down beside him, he asks them to move so he can get out. Mike gets back up, opens up his stuff, and can't find what he's looking for, all the while apologizing to everyone around him for him taking so long. Eventually, he finally has everything he needs, and the flight finishes boarding and takes off.

Mike has a big smile on his face and is really excited to be going on his trip and can't wait to get there. He's a kind and nice gentleman and seems friendly to everyone around him. He's striking up conversations with anyone that will speak to him and is completely and totally oblivious to how annoying his behavior has been to the frequent flyers.

Mike is the personification of every single thing that business and frequent travelers hate. Whether I am traveling for work or pleasure, the actual travel process, as in going from plane to plane and place to place, is the part of traveling that I loathe. Once I leave home, the only thing I am thinking about is getting to my destination. I have said before that many times the "journey" is part of the fun, but the actual mechanics of air travel is not. This is the one instance where the destination is all that matters, and the journey is just a means of getting there. The "journey" to me is nothing more than lines filled with people like Mike who are holding me up from getting me where I want to go. Sure, I know that Mike isn't going to prevent the plane from leaving with his minor eccentricities. However, it still feels like a delay when all I want to do is get to my seat and be left alone as I wait for the plane to take off.

For folks like Mike and his friends who are traveling with him, the whole thing is just one fun experience. That novelty of travel quickly wears off when you are doing it several times a month. After a while, you come to realize that although it's great to be able to see these different places you are visiting, it's not really a lot of fun getting there. When you hear someone say that getting there is half the fun, ask them about that after they've had to fly to and from home 25 times a year.

I'll then get friends who say that it must be nice to see the world on someone else's dime. Yes, there are obvious perks to being able to travel when someone else is paying the bills. However, when you go for work, it's not a vacation. There's no sight-seeing like there is when you don't have work obligations. I spend my entire day standing in front of a class of students delivering training. My days usually run anywhere from 9am to 5:30pm, depending on the client. By the time I am done, I am exhausted, my feet hurt, and many times I've got a sore throat from talking so much. A lot of times, the last thing I feel like doing is going out and seeing anything. At the end of your workday, do you feel like going out? There have been so many times I would think that I should go out and try to see something. I am often in new places I've never been to before, so I should go see something, shouldn't I?

As I write this paragraph, I'm sitting in a hotel room in San Diego, California. It's a city I've never had the chance to experience previously. I really wanted to explore the area tonight, but my feet and legs are so sore from standing all day that I opted to stay in my room and watch TV and work on my book. Plus, I'm suffering from a 4hr time difference from home, so jetlag is still setting in. As much as I want to explore the city, my body tells me to take the night off and rest. I can explore the area tomorrow (which I did).

Add to that the fact that most museums, galleries, or other exciting places to see (typical tourist stuff) are all closed by the time my day is done. That means that the only real time I get to see anything is on the day I arrive after I have checked into a hotel. If I am lucky, I might book a vacation day or two ahead of or after my work trip, but those meals and hotels are on me, not work. So the amount of time I actually get to "see" anything is minimal because I spend my days working. Yes, work is paying for me to be in London, Dublin, Sydney, or New York, but they aren't paying me to be a tourist. The only time I might get extra days covered by work is when it's an overseas flight, and additional nights are cheaper than flights. A single day can make a flight $1000 less expensive in some instances. I have had occurrences where I had to stay the weekend, so in those rare cases, it has been advantageous to have work pay for my hotels and meals.

On top of that, there's the constant fear of flights being delayed or, worse, canceled. Cancellations and delays are a part of the entire air travel industry. For those who don't fly often, they tend to think that these things are done for no logical reason. I have heard many people gripe about delays and cancellations. Sure, I hate them too, but they are a reality of air travel, and you can either shake your fists at the sky, thinking it will help or accept them.

Nothing sucks more than sitting at a gate and then finding out your flight has been delayed or canceled, and it may throw off your entire trip. I once had a flight delayed because the toilet was frozen. A colleague of mine had his flight canceled because the flight attendant didn't have the demo seat belt to do the safety walkthrough. The first leg on my Galapagos vacation was canceled because the pilot informed the passengers that he couldn't turn a knob counterclockwise. Because of that one cancellation, I showed up a day late for my tour.

At the peak of my traveling, I would average about 8-10 flights a month, depending on how busy I am. During the summer, I had 16 different flights, to four cities, in two countries, with two other towns being used for connections. Dealing with security lines, delays, cancellations, dumb travelers, and many other air-related follies is physically and mentally draining. The stress of flying is hard on the head and running your ass off from one end of an airport to another is physically tiring. The last time I had to run for a flight, I ran all the way from the US connections portion of Pearson airport to the Canadian side in a few minutes. It was bad enough that when I got on the plane, I actually had the flight attendants a bit scared for my health as I looked pretty winded. I was definitely having difficulties breathing, and the sweat was pouring off of me. (Speaking of which, I really need to get in better shape). Then, after finally making it to the plane, we sat at the gate for 45 minutes. I still would have missed the flight if I hadn't run across the airport, but then to get there and literally sit on the plane for that long before we left was extremely frustrating.

On a plane in Newark, New Jersey, we taxied out to the runway for takeoff. After several other aircraft took off, we took our position on the runway. We were waiting for the confirmation from the tower for takeoff. It seemed to be taking longer than usual, and I had a sinking feeling in my stomach that something was wrong. Sure enough, the pilot came on and told us the flight had been canceled. I ended up staying in Newark until the next night to catch my flight home. There wasn't anything I could do about it, but it was still extremely frustrating. I've even been on a plane that started to take off and then slammed on the brakes to stop, and then the flight was canceled.

This brings me to a pet peeve I have about air travel. Living in Canada, I have to fly either Air Canada (AC) or Westjet (WJ). AC is a larger airline and therefore offers many more connections and flights than WJ. When it comes to customer service, you always hear people complain about AC. Lost luggage, crappy cancellation or delay service, and countless other complaints always seem to surface with AC but rarely with WJ. So the assumption is that AC is a horrible airline. It bothers me to no end to hear people complain about AC, or any airline for that matter, when they don't realize that there are so many passengers out there who do just fine. How many passengers does AC fly in a single day? And of those passengers, how many of them have their luggage lost, or have a canceled or delayed flight? The percentage will always be small because of pure volume. Yet you never see people talk about that. You only hear people complain.

One person's bad experiences with an airline do not equate to the entire company being terrible. You might be dealing with bad luck, or someone who just likes to complain. Take it all in context as there is always more than one side to a story.

In one instance, I was booked on a flight to get home around noon time. For whatever reason, my flight was canceled, and Air Canada put me on a plane to get me back around midnight. I really needed to be home by lunchtime. The first person from Air Canada I spoke to could get me on a flight that would get me in around 2pm, which was better but not ideal. Another agent then came over and asked me to hold on for a moment. She went on her terminal and did something and eventually came back and told me she could get me into Moncton by 11:30 and asked if that was ok.

I said this was more than acceptable but was curious how the other agent couldn't find any flights. She told me that there were no Air Canada flights available, but there was a Westjet flight that got in at 11:30, and she put me on that, no charge. I was perplexed, but sure enough, the airlines do have that ability. I thanked her and went into the other terminal.

Those are the kinds of stories that you don't hear very often because people tend to focus on negative content. You also have no idea that perhaps a flight was canceled because the aircraft had become unsafe. Would you rather the plane explode or fall apart mid-air, or not be able to land, or be inconvenienced by being delayed? It's a much larger picture than what most people think of out of the gate.

I cannot stress enough that when it comes to traveling, you need to be very mindful of what you need to do, where you need to be, and how your actions will affect others around you. Try to be as quick and courteous as you can, and also try to remember that when things go wrong, it could be far worse.

Floating in the Sand

In November of 2013, my wife and I took a trip to Jordan. We had wanted to celebrate turning 40 by going to see the Great Pyramids of Giza in Egypt. At that time, there was a lot of political unrest going on, and the tour was canceled. We had initially planned to spend a few days in Jordan after Egypt to see Petra and the Dead Sea. With Egypt now canceled, we modified the trip to make Jordan the primary destination. We spent a couple days in Frankfurt, Germany, then headed off to Jordan on a Monday night.

We landed in Amman, Jordan, the capital city, around 2am. After getting through customs, obtaining our luggage, and finding our ride, we headed off to our hotel, which was located in the nearby city of Madaba. That ride alone was an unsettling experience. We got into a car with a man who had been sent by the hotel. He quickly got us out of the airport area and took some side roads on his way to Madaba. It was pitch black with nothing other than a handful of small fires to be seen. At about 3:00am local time, the only thing we could spot from the car was broken down cars and the occasional dead animal. It looked very much like a barren wasteland. Was this how our vacation was going to start?

Now, you have to understand that Jordan was about as foreign a place as we had ever been to. We had read up a lot about the country and knew that we would be relatively safe. With what had happened in Egypt, and all the news we hear about regarding the middle-east, it was hard not to have preconceptions. We both sat in the back of the car, a little frazzled, but excited at the same time.

About 30 minutes after leaving the airport, we got to the hotel and checked in, and we were quite surprised by the small single beds that filled the main living area. We didn't really care as all we wanted was to sleep. Our plan was to get up, see the highlights of Madaba, and then make our way to the Dead Sea later that same day as we had made reservations at a Holiday Inn resort nearby.

When we woke up, we could now see outside. Between the overcast skies and all the pale, stone, vanilla looking buildings, it soon began to feel a bit more foreign than we had thought. We had breakfast and then decided to go for a walk. I had brought my handheld GPS and had a vague idea of where the visitor's center was, so we went on our way. Once we left the hotel, however, we really started to see how dirty the place was. Garbage was all over the streets, and we must have seen at least three or four dead cats on the edges of the sidewalk as we wandered around.

Apart from the mess, the other thing that stood out was the smell. To this day, there are times when I am out and about on my regular day, and I catch a scent of something and am immediately reminded of Jordan. There was always the smell of something burning. Not a bad smell, but more like an intense version of a campfire that sticks on your clothes after roasting marshmallows. That smell of something being burned seemed to permeate throughout the country, no matter where we were. It was the first thing I noticed the moment I stepped outside the hotel.

Out the door and to the left, we wandered down the street. The GPS gave us excellent directions as to where the visitor center was. Still, as we walked, we started to feel a bit uncomfortable with the attention the locals were giving us. Many people seemed to stare as we walked, and we began to wonder if my wife should have her body covered up more than it was. The literature I had read said she was fine dressing casually. But, we really started to wonder, judging by what we saw. We were somewhat nervous as we walked around and got some strange looks from the locals. When we finally did reach the visitor's center, the women working there assured us that we had nothing to worry about. There was nothing to be concerned about with regards to our safety or Tamara having to cover up. From there, we headed towards the central part of town to do some exploring. Once the locals assured us of our safety, we never thought about it again. All the worries and preconceptions we had from the night before had disappeared, and we could enjoy the rest of our trip in peace.

We did get to see some of the fantastic mosaics for which Madaba and Jordan are known for. The intricate work of some of these pieces was astonishing. Still, it was even more so when we were shown some of the work that was literally hundreds to several thousand years old. I had seen mosaics before but nothing to the extent that these people were creating. We did a little walk around the town center then came back to the hotel to check out, store our bags, arrange a drive, and head back out. We visited a church with an old mosaic floor that had been uncovered years ago. It was pretty amazing stuff to see. We watched a guy fill a bottle with colored sand draw using sand and glue to create a sunset with our names in the sand. We then had some food where I ate some sort of weird chicken dish with a white paste sauce that was not to my liking. I somehow managed to muddle through. I found out later that the actual meal is called shawarma. I had heard that name before but couldn't recall where from. Turns out, it was from watching the end credits scene in the original Avengers movie. After having lunch, we wandered through an outdoor shopping market, looking at much of the local handiwork. Like the mosaics, much of what these people could produce was quite a sight to see, but that wasn't the most surprising thing about the area.

What stood out the most were the people themselves. Even though we initially felt like everyone was staring at us, every single person we met was so welcoming and friendly. They would ask where we were from and what brought us to their town. Never did we experience any sort of aggressive behavior or attitude towards us. During our time in Jordan, there was only one instance where we had a miscommunication with a local. Beyond that, the people were amazingly friendly.

We took some more photos and then headed back to our hotel, where our ride to the Dead Sea was waiting for us. Turns out, we'd see a lot more before we got there.

Our driver knew we were just seeing the sights, so he made a few stops on the way to the Dead Sea. He took us to some sort of Jordanian museum where there were many replicas of famous biblical stories that were known about the area. We didn't have to pay to get in, and honestly, it was kind of tacky. It was nice to see that they had put this together, but it really was just a bunch of fake people set in some of these scenes depicting the earlier days of Jordan.

One memorable part of the museum was where we put in a few pieces of stone to a large mosaic that was being submitted to Guinness as the largest in the world. We put our names on a couple of squares and glued them into place. I have since tried to find the mosaic in the Guinness Book of World Records but have not seen it appear yet.

The driver continued on his way along the road towards the Dead Sea. Now, it was just desert on either side of this road, and the filth and garbage that we saw in Madaba didn't stop at the city boundary. It continued everywhere, which was very unfortunate. We would learn later from our tour of Jerusalem and Bethlehem that this is not an uncommon practice. In Israel, certain cities have sections dedicated to various religious groups. For some of them, the neighborhoods would be quite filthy and covered in the garbage. Still, the actual insides of their homes were impeccably maintained. It's apparently some sort of cultural difference that was most notable in that region of the world. As our driver continued on, he made another stop for us at a place called Mount Nebo.

According to Christian legend, Mount Nebo is where Moses looked out into the desert and saw the Promised Land. We took some photos of the beautiful area, and I cracked a joke about Moses using the pipes to bring water to the locals. We didn't stay too long, but we did see a pretty beautiful view of the valley from there. As someone who is not overly devout to a particular faith, the visit here was the first of several sites we would visit with religious history. Looking out and seeing the desert and knowing that this was a place that was depicted in the Bible, it gave me a moment of pause. I grew up hearing many stories from the Bible. Although my own path of spirituality has led me in a different direction. I could certainly appreciate the magnitude of what it meant to be standing in a place many people would revel in.

We arrived at the Holiday Inn Dead Sea resort right around suppertime. Word was that the beach closed at sunset, and Tamara really wanted to get into the water before that happened. As quickly as we could, we dropped our bags in our room and went off to the beach to see what the big deal was about.

If you're unfamiliar with the Dead Sea, it's mostly a salt lake bordered by Jordan, Israel, and Palestine. It has a salinity of about

34%, which makes it one of the saltiest bodies of water in the world. Due to this salinity and the density of the water, it's virtually impossible to sink in it. Well known for many health products that are derived from the contents of the sea, it's also said the water and nearby mud contain many healing properties. In researching Jordan, the Dead Sea came up frequently as a "must-see" place. Even colleagues of mine who had been to Jordan before insisted that I had to check it out. Once we got to our room, it was off to the beach to see what this was all about.

The water was cold, but you could very clearly see on the surface of the water a sort of film that seemed to glisten. We knew the salt content was high, but it was interesting to notice that you can actually *see* it. We walked out just a bit, and before we knew it, the salt was lifting us up. It is not like anything else you will ever experience. As someone who has lived near the Atlantic Ocean for most of my life, I can tell you that floating in the water back home is nothing like this. You have *no* control over *not* hovering. In fact, at one point, I stood in the water, straight up, not able to touch the ground because the water just pushed me up. You could roll around without issue and would never sink. Both of us turned and twisted and did anything and everything we could to try and sink down more, but it just wasn't going to happen. I did make the mistake of at one point, opening my eyes while underwater. That made for a very uncomfortable few minutes. The experience of having that much salty water into one's eyes is not one I would recommend. Floating there with the sun going down made for a perfect way to finish off the "experiences" of the day. We got out, took a quick swim in the regular pool, and then went to have supper. But not before we'd enjoy some delightful dinner entertainment.

We opted to have supper outside at one of the restaurants at the hotel. What we had seen after arriving there was that stray cats were actually the norm. We saw several of them while exploring the property, and when we sat at our table, a few came over. As cat people, Tamara and I didn't mind it at all. We did not, however, expect that after a few minutes, there would be more. At some point, I think there were as many as seven cats around the dining area. We smiled and just took it all in as part of the experience of being somewhere foreign. One of the staff told us that the cats are part of the area, and they have tried to get rid of them, but they just keep coming back.

Now the funny thing was that these cats were hungry. They are strays and are looking for any food you might have, and they are not afraid to make it known. We had a couple of them paw at us and meow but never acted aggressively. However, for a few select other people, the cats jumped on the chairs, the table, and even swatted a couple of the other guests. It was even more entertaining because the cats seem to sense which guests were cat people and which ones weren't because they only went after the people who hated cats. Tamara and I sat there and laughed as one older couple got pretty mad and was yelling at the animals. The food was not anything spectacular, but the entertainment was excellent.

When we got up the next morning, we knew we would be leaving by noonish, so Tamara wanted to get in another float plus a mud bath. We went down to the beach again and did a bit of bobbing in the water and also took a walk along the shore, where Tamara snagged a bit of mud and salt to bring back home. To finish it all up, Tamara got covered from one end to the other in the famous Dead Sea mud. For me, it didn't feel any different than regular mud, but it was pretty cool. We cleaned up, checked out, and then started on our ride towards Wadi Musa, where we'd have our encounter with Petra.

As a side note to that particular part of our trip, the resort required you to use a "towel card" to get a towel to use outside. If you didn't return your towels, then you would be charged for each towel you used/kept. Unbeknownst to me, Tamara put two towels in our bag and then "pretended" like we had lost them. To this day, she still swears that those two towels are the best ones we have in the house. Now and then, I'll spot the tags on the towels, notice the writing is in Arabic, and be reminded of where they came from.

Getting from the Dead Sea to Wadi Musa and Petra was about four hours by car along the Jordan Valley Highway. We knew the drive would be long, but it was the only way to get there. The same driver who had driven us to the Dead Sea came back and picked us up to drive us to Petra. He was a fantastic driver and knew all of the best spots to stop to see the best views of the valleys. One of my all-time favorite photos was taken during that drive when we stopped at one lookout point. The picture is nothing more than two chairs sitting opposite of each other with a small chess table between them. They sat at the very edge of a cliff that dropped down into the Dead Sea. The photo is strikingly beautiful.

Some of the more memorable spots along our journey were to a "cave" motel. There was this little shop along one of the small little villages we drove through that was actually a store built into an old cave. While Tamara was looking at the jewelry, I wandered around the area a bit. I found an actual motel that was inside of the cave. The beds themselves were made of stone, and you could get a room there if you wanted.

Then we were taken to Shobak Castle in the middle of the desert. We were greeted by a friendly gentleman who wanted to be our guide to the castle. He led us around, showing us this very long and dark deep hole where they used to get water. We saw places where they hung criminals and all kinds of other noteworthy aspects to the castle. His tour and knowledge of the castle were great, but he really seemed to take a liking to my wife. Every time I turned around, he put his arms around her, holding her, and it made me very uncomfortable. We got through it and made our way out of there, making several stops along the highway to take pictures of the desert and views. So pale but so beautiful at the same time. While on our way to Wadi Musa, our driver made arrangements to get tickets to see Petra at Night. When we finally pulled into our hotel, he stuck his arm out the window, and two tickets were mysteriously placed in his hand, and then he put them in ours, and that was it. The ride was done, and we would begin our adventures in Petra that evening.

For those unfamiliar with what Petra is, I'd suggest a quick Google search, and you'll find yourself pretty amazed by what you'll see and read. If you saw Indiana Jones and the Last Crusade, you've seen part of Petra. In the movie, Indy and his dad ride horses down something called the "canyon of the crescent moon." They eventually reach an entrance to an old temple. That was shot at what is known as The Treasury in Petra. Of all things we would encounter in Jordan, I'd rate The Treasury as being at the top of my "must-see" list.

After we got checked into our room, we opted to go for a little walk. Across the street from the hotel, we found the entrance to Petra. There was a pile of small shops there with folks trying to sell you pretty much anything. There was even a little shop called "The Indiana Jones Gift Shop." We walked by one of the stores, and a guy insisted we come in and dress us up. He proceeded to put one of the headwraps on Tamara and me and took our picture.

After waiting for a little while, we started to follow the crowd into Petra for the Petra at Night show. We walked, and walked, and walked, and walked some more through a long walkway and passageway lit by candles. Because there was so little light (which, of course, is part of the whole experience), we didn't see much until after 30-40 minutes of walking when we finally got to "The Treasury."

The Treasury is really this giant carved out temple of sorts into the side of a red-ish/tan colored rock face. The lower portion of the "entrance" looks similar to a Roman-style bank with a set of six columns, three on each side of the doorway, which is really just a big hole into nothing. Above that were three sets of two columns with other decorative items at the top of each set. All of this is carved into the actual rock itself. It's enormous to look at, and in the dark, the details were obscured but still quite striking to see. In front of The Treasury was a sea of candles, and then the music began. We parked ourselves at a picnic table and watched the show.

It's hard to remember exactly the order of how things went. Still, I remember a man playing a sort of flute instrument that seemed to go on *forever*. It was charming to enjoy the local music, but I am sure he played one song that lasted at least 30 minutes. After a while, I was getting bored and just wanted it to be over with. I didn't want to be insensitive about it, but it really did seem to drag on forever. I'm also sure that having spent the bulk of the day in a car didn't help either. At some other point, they had a man come out and tell us a few stories about the history of Petra and what we would see. Eventually, the music and lecture ended, and we wandered around for a while. Then I made a minor pit stop just on one side of the monument to give Tamara and me an unforgettable memory.

Our anniversary was in October, and typically every year, we've had a "dance" to our song. Yes, it's kind of cheesy, but it's been our thing since we got married. That year, however, I purposely didn't remind her about the dance or bring it up. Sure enough, we didn't bother when our anniversary date came along.

I found a quiet little corner, dug out my phone, and played our song. As the music played, we danced together under the moonlight in the middle of Petra. Not the most popular romantic location for a dance, but we aren't the most conventional couple either. This was a nice little sidebar to our touring and an excellent memory for both of us. After that, we headed back to the hotel, where we really did crash for the night as the next day would be quite busy.

We woke up bright and early, packed our small day trip bags, grabbed the hiking poles, and headed off to see Petra. I fired up my GPS and wanted to track exactly where we went and how long it took us. According to the track, we hiked about 15.5Km for over 8 hours. Now keep in mind that a lot of that time was also sightseeing as well. If it were pure hiking, we would have covered a lot more territory, but what we did cover was quite something.

We started down the same path we had been down the night before, but this time we could actually see things. It was a long path with cool stone caves on either side and a defined lane for horses. We eventually came to a sort of turning point where we entered what is known as the "Siq." This was basically a very long and narrow passageway between tall rocks that we had to follow until we would hit the start of Petra itself.

Wandering along the path, we walked and took pictures and admired a lot of things. The size of the Siq and the rocks around us were pretty breathtaking. We saw a few donkeys and carriages carrying people, but we kept on foot. You could also spot some little kids playing and trying to sell the tourists some small trinkets.

Eventually, we came to the end of the Siq, and the Treasury peaked out behind it. I got really excited as I knew we were getting there, and just as I was about to bounce off a wall, it all came into sight.

To see the Treasury in the day is quite something. There's nothing quite like looking at an ancient Jordanian structure that's been sitting there for more than 2000 years. I took a pile of photos and just soaked in as much as I could see. Tamara and I walked around a little bit. Eventually, we worked our way past the Treasury to some of the other small tombs and made our way towards the central part of Petra. I actually had no idea how vast Petra was, and once we started down that path, it became pretty clear that the size of this place was far beyond what we had expected.

There were many people around and a lot of tourists and a lot of people trying to sell you horse or camel rides. We said we would stick to being on foot until we couldn't walk anymore. We also checked out a few small little vendors who kept insisting that their prices were the best. "Only 2 dinar," we heard many, many times. (Dinar is the currency in Jordan).

Eventually, we opted to climb the steps to the "High Place of Sacrifice," which is basically on top of the mountain. Tamara paid for a local donkey to go up as she didn't think she could do the hike. They started up the steps just behind me. Within 5 minutes of getting on the donkey, Tamara almost went headfirst onto the ground as she slipped off the side of the animal. That was enough for her to say no thanks to the donkey and try the hike anyway. The hike up for me was challenging, but the hiking poles really helped, and you just took your time. Before you knew it, you were up high enough that local merchants on the mountain were trying to sell you stuff. Tamara was slower than I, but she took her time, and like a real champ, she made it all the way to the top. We were both pretty proud of the fact that we got up there on our own.

Once there, we had a pretty remarkable view of the entire area, including down where we had just come from. We headed on to the place of high sacrifice, which was an area where at one time, many animals were sacrificed, and their blood would drain off. One of the locals gave us the full rundown on what it was all about. Tamara made friends with a local woman there who was quite fascinated by her. When we finally came down off the spot where the high place was, there was a sitting area. The woman showed Tamara her baby, and they talked for a bit before we moved on.

A point of interest here is that I managed to find two geocaches in that particular area. Tamara's new friend helped me find one, and the other one was stuck in a rock wall overlooking the backend of Petra. Even in the middle of what felt like nowhere, geocaches could be found.

We started down the back way and going down for me was more comfortable than going up. Before we knew it, we were looking at an old garden tomb along with other tombs on the ground. We came to a spot where we had to decide which direction to go. Based on where we were, it wasn't overly evident which direction we should take. This is where the GPS came in handy.

The GPS had drawn a breadcrumb trail on the map to show us where we had already been, so as we looked at it from where we were, the track showed that we should go right, but there was no clear path as to where to go. So, trusting what the GPS said, we walked where it seemed the most logical to walk and hoped for the best. A little weirded out, I tried not to think about it and just kept following the GPS until it showed us getting closer to the track line we had already been on. Before we knew it, we could see down below where people were, and then we spotted some familiar spots from where we had started. We made our way back to the road and stopped for a minute.

I'd like to mention that in this case, having the GPS with me essentially saved us. There was a sign giving us vague directions to places we had never heard of. Exhaustion was starting to set in, and we pondered if we had enough to keep going. There was enough gas in our tanks to keep rolling but had we followed the sign to another part of the city, we would have had a much longer trek back to the Siq. Having that track line on the GPS showing us where we had been made it much easier to know exactly where we needed to go. Even our cell phones didn't have that capability or battery life to help us in that situation.

Tamara was feeling a bit sore, but I was determined to see a few more tombs that I wanted to take some photos of. So, she sat and rested while I made my way over to a few more monuments. Tamara made some new friends who insisted on getting their photos taken with her since she was the one who looked different from them.

After I got back, we worked our way back to the Treasury and made one more stop at the Theatre. This was the last thing I wanted to see while I was there, so I took a few more photos, and then we started the trek back to the hotel, through the Treasury and the Siq. By the time we got to the hotel, we had spent a whole 8 hours out and about hiking. We were dead tired, but man, the things we saw would never compare to anything else, ever.

When we got up the next morning, we had breakfast and made our way to Wadi Rum. Wadi Rum was something I had never heard of, but one of the guys I work with had been to Jordan before and recommended it as something to do. It's a protected part of the Jordanian desert. Many people go out there to see the mountain areas and desert and camp out under the stars. This seemed like a very relaxing way to experience the desert, so I signed us up for a night there.

Years later, I would find out that many movies get filmed in Wadi Rum because of the look and feel of the desert. The Martian with Matt Damon shot a lot of the Mars footage in Wadi Rum. We actually took a taxi from Petra to Wadi Rum, which was quite a long drive. When we finally got there, we got on an open back "jeep" and set sail for the desert. Now this jeep was not an actual jeep. Instead, it was a pickup truck with a sort of half-canvas on top of it. Not great for coverage and not great for all-terrain driving, but is apparently the norm in that area. We were driven to a shack-like building, which was our first stop. Tamara had some tea while I snapped some photos.

From that point forward, we went from one notable location to another with our guide, Rakan. He took us to a wicked sand dune, which we climbed up and took some photos. He also brought us to a couple of places that had ancient writing on the rocks. At one point, we ended up at another dune where people were using a snowboard to "slide" down the side of the dune. It was pretty funny to watch. While we sat there and watched them try to go down the hill, our guide tried to get his truck fixed as it had died. Neither one of us were too worried about being stuck out there as we were just enjoying the experience and soaking up everything we could see around us.

Once the vehicle was mobile again, he took us exploring some more to a small canyon and rocks, which were pretty cool. Eventually, we ended up having lunch in the desert and then heading onward to our camp. Just before hitting camp, we stopped at this "cow" rock. Our guide showed off his climbing skills as he got up to the top and waved down to us. We took some photos and then went to the camp.

Turns out, our camp was not just tenting in the desert. We had a little hut with two beds where we stashed our stuff. Our guide prepared our supper along with his friend, and two other folks who were staying at the camp. The other local, his name was Omar, was telling us stories of him and his dad hunting. Turns out, they hunt with machine guns here. He showed us a few pictures, and it was pretty funny to see someone with a machine gun in their hand while trying to hunt for the Jordanian version of a deer. At one point, one of the other visitors said, "Omar, you look like a terrorist." My eyes jumped out of my head, thinking that was something you just don't say. Surprisingly enough, Omar paused for a moment then laughed as he said he did kind of look like a terrorist.

They finished the night off by going outside, setting off some small fireworks on the ground and on the top of one of the rocks. Tamara and I took a walk around one of the big hills and enjoyed the sunset in the desert. It was so quiet and so peaceful that it was weird not to hear much of anything. Add to that the fact that there was no light except the moonlight and stars that you really could see the entire sky.

We crashed for the night and woke up in the morning, ready to go. Our bags were taken for us, and we were put on camels, which we would ride back into town. Now here's the thing about riding a camel: It feels kind of cool for about 5 minutes, and then afterward, your ass starts to hurt. It is not comfy to be on for very long. I sat crisscrossed on the camel and switched positions often to try and be comfortable, but it really didn't help. By the end of those two hours, my rear end hurt some bad and would continue to be uncomfortable for the next few days.

The ride back into town took about two hours. Still, the funniest thing about that entire experience was the fact that here we are riding camels in the desert, and our guide is talking on his cell phone. I managed to snap a photo of him on his phone in the middle of the desert, although when I went to find it for this book, I discovered you really can't see the phone from the photo. From there, we snagged a ride over to Aqaba, where we would spend our last night in Jordan before working our way back to the capital on our journey home.

Aqaba itself was just a sort of beach town. Not a lot to do there, but we did wander around a bit and get some food. The hotel was pretty nice, but security was a bit of a pain in the ass because of language issues. It would turn out to be the only negative experience we encountered with the locals. For starters, many of the hotels in the Middle East and Asia have metal detectors, and x-ray machines at the entrance, much like you experience at the airport. We had gone to Pizza Hut for supper and brought back some leftovers. When we tried to go through security, the security guy wouldn't let us bring the food. So I said okay and put it on the machine. After I went through the metal detector, he starts yelling at me in Arabic about the pizza. He apparently said I couldn't bring it into the hotel, but he didn't tell me what to do with it. I tried to explain that if I can't bring it in, what do you want me to do? The disagreement got a bit heated, and then the hotel bellboy came over and talked to him, and the security guy just barked something at me and told me to take the pizza.

We took the bus down to the beach to do some snorkeling in the Red Sea, which was a big highlight for Tamara as she had never snorkeled before. I had not been able to do snorkeling previously because I kept panicking when my face was in the water. This time, I took my time and managed to figure out a way that worked for me. Once I got it, it was easy from there on in. We spent a few hours exploring the reefs and enjoying the sun before heading back to the hotel.

That night, we took a taxi to the Aqaba airport and caught a flight back to Amman, where we had begun our journey through Jordan. The experience of flying the local carrier at a local airport was an interesting one. For starters, I wasn't allowed to have the carabiner from my GPS in my carry-on bag. They really dug through our entire luggage and asked many questions, but we were eventually let through. Although that was a little unsettling, it had nothing on what I saw while the flight was in the air.

Aqaba to Amman is only an hour or so by air. It travels from the southernmost point of the country north. I was on the right, which would have been the east side of the plane at a window seat. It was midnight when we left, so everything was pitch black. As we are flying, I start to see these flashes of light off in the distance, which at first, I didn't think anything of it, but after a while, some of them were pretty big. I then realized that these were explosions. From everything I could tell, it looked like weaponry of some kind that was going off in the middle of the night. I got pretty freaked out as I had never seen explosions on the ground from the air like that. I have no idea what they were or where they came from, but it was kind of freaky to see. I asked several locals about it and never really got a good explanation as to what it actually was. It may have been Jordanian or Saudi military exercises. However, it was still a bit scary to see from the air. We got to Amman, snagged a cab to our hotel, proceeded to crash for a few hours before our last day of sightseeing.

Given that Amman was less than 50km from Israel, Tamara and I opted to take a day tour of Jerusalem and Bethlehem just to be able to say we were there. I may not be a Christian, but to be that close, you kind of have to go see it just to say you were there. I will say that I am glad I got to go, but unless work sent me there for business, it's unlikely I will return.

We had arranged a tour, so we got picked up at the hotel and driven to the Allenby Bridge. This is a bridge that goes between Jordan and Israel. When you get to the Jordan side, they check you in and **take your passport**. They don't just look at it, they keep it. They then load you onto a bus, and once on the bus, they give you your passport back. You then cross the bridge, and in the process go through, I believe it was 5 or 6 security checkpoints on the way. Once across the bridge, you go through two more sets of security screenings: One for your luggage and one for immigration. Once out, our guide was there and picked us up for our tour, but it seemed to take forever to get there. The total distance from where the cab dropped us off to where the guide picked us up was just over 4km, yet it took several hours to traverse that distance.

Our guide in Israel was fantastic, but the overall experience there was very disappointing. It's for this reason why I opted not to write an entire chapter about that part of my travel history. The biggest thing about the whole experience was that Tamara and I only knew of the biblical Jerusalem and Bethlehem, a far cry from the real thing. Neither of us was well versed in the modern-day versions of these places. Both places were excessively overcrowded and **very** hectic. It was kind of insane how busy it was in that part of the world. There were so many people there to see so much of what it had to offer. The massive crowds were somewhat intimidating and overwhelming. I've since been to places like India where there are vast masses of people, but it still doesn't compare to what I experienced in Israel.

We did get to see the supposed birthplace and deathbed of Jesus and did get to see the famous Western, AKA Wailing Wall. We also saw Sheppard's fields, which was kind of cool. We took some photos, but a lot of the interiors were hard to capture on camera. Plus, with so many people around, it was kind of crazy. The most unsettling part of it all was how so many were *so* emotional about being there. There was a stone tablet of some sort that Jesus had allegedly blessed, and many people wanted to touch it or pray on it. The tomb where Jesus was buried was also another spot with a huge long line of people just waiting to get inside. Despite this not being part of my belief system, I could still appreciate the value and importance of places like this. Still, the sheer emotion displayed by people visiting there was very overwhelming and unsettling at times.

Another interesting thing was that we had two guides. The first one couldn't take us to Bethlehem because that's considered part of Palestine, and he wasn't allowed to go there. No security this time, but we did switch vehicles. The second guide was adequate but not great. He really tried to push us to buy souvenirs at some shop he must have been associated with as he insisted, we stop there on our way out. There were some beautiful items in the store, especially some of the handmade wooden crafts. The hefty price tags that exceeded $1,000 US dollars in some cases definitely stalled any chance of us buying anything of value. I bought a small Christmas decoration to hang from my tree to say that it had come from the actual Bethlehem. Tamara and I stopped just before going back to Jerusalem to have the driver take a photo of us under a sign welcoming visitors to the city.

We finished the day off with a ride back to the bridge, where we went through the same sort of long hassle about getting back into Jordan. From there, we hit the hotel and crashed, and then headed to the airport for our 2am flight. Before we knew it, we were back in our own home, and it was all over.

This was a trip that was supposed to be one thing but turned into something else. For both Tamara and I, it was a fantastic experience. It was also one of the first trips where I was conscious of just "taking it all in." There were plenty of instances where one could have become frustrated or annoyed by little nuances. Still, instead of looking at them negatively, I chose to just soak it in as part of being in that place. I think for me, that's one of the biggest reasons why I enjoyed it so much. Since then, I have made a point of merely emerging myself in the local mindset when visiting some of these foreign places and have found it to be quite something. When you just take a deep breath and marvel at what is around you, the experience becomes so much more than just a tour of some foreign land.

If you ever have the chance to see Jordan, go. Don't hesitate and just go see it. It was indeed an excellent place to visit and would recommend it to anyone.

Peaks, Valleys, & Plains

In early 2014, my friend and I had been hired to assist with the production of the TV show The Amazing Race Canada. Our geocaching organization, Cache Up NB, was asked to help the TV program with one of the stops the players would encounter on their race during the second season of the show. While we were ecstatic to be invited, we had to keep our involvement a secret until September of that year. We were told that we would need to be available for on-camera work and the actual detour stop on May 12th & May 13th. Being asked to assist with this TV show was a massive deal for both of us. So there was nothing that was going to get in our way of participating.

Then along came April of that same year, and my boss asked me if I wanted to go to Johannesburg, South Africa (J'Burg), for a one-week work assignment. These kinds of trips are rare to come up, so when they do, we jump on the opportunity to go. There was just one problem: I had to be there for May 12th. I really wanted to go, but I also knew that I wanted to do The Amazing Race Canada, and it seemed it was going to be one or the other. I asked if there was any way that the class could be moved to a week earlier due to a prior commitment. She said she couldn't make any promises but would ask. A few nervous days later, she returned to tell me that she could get the training moved and approved my vacation time before the work assignment. I was literally jumping for joy as now I would get both the TV show work and a free trip to Africa.

Knowing that I might never get the chance to go back there, I opted to take a week of vacation and do a safari in Kruger National Park. I was initially going to go by myself. When I mentioned to my wife about her coming with me, it wasn't long before I had a travel companion. It also turns out that deciding to bring her with me would allow me to cross off the #1 item from my own bucket list: The Great Pyramids of Giza.

When I searched for flights for my wife, the cheapest one available actually had a 12hr layover in Cairo, Egypt. I bought the ticket immediately and then made my own travel arrangements to match hers. It was a weird route to get to South Africa from Moncton, but the price was within my client's budget, and I couldn't say no to going to Egypt.

You see, when I was in the 6th grade, I was given a history assignment on ancient Egypt. It was one of the only school assignments that I actually spent a considerable amount of extra work on. It included countless visits to the library with my mom, research on pharaohs and tombs, and many nights printing as clearly as I could. It paid off in the end when I earned a 100% mark. That project binder still sits somewhere in my mother's basement and always brings a smile to my face when I think about how much work I put into it. Because of all the things I learned about Egypt in my grade school days, I developed an intense desire to visit the Great Pyramids someday. It was at the top of my bucket list for many years, and now I had a chance to finally cross it off.

On May 5th, 2014, we left Moncton and headed to Cairo via Montreal, then New York City. I had made plans for a day tour of the city, including the pyramids, and we met our guide at the airport. After grabbing our luggage, we got into the car and headed straight for Giza, where the pyramids were waiting.

The first thing I can tell you about Cairo is that it's a busy city and a lot larger than you might realize. It is in the middle of the desert but yet still surrounded by industrial buildings. It's also very odd to see the pyramids in the distance while we were inside the city. What you don't see in tourist magazines or TV shows is that the pyramids are actually right in the middle of a metropolis. They aren't isolated in the middle of the desert, as you might think.

We parked the car, got out, went through the gates, and there they were. This was 30 years in the making. I stood there and paused for a moment, took a bunch of photos, and then started to explore. We did a lap around The Great Pyramid (also known as Pyramid of Khufu) to get a sense of how big they were and see as much as possible. We went into one small chamber on one of the side pyramids where we snapped a few pictures and just reveled in the reality of where we were.

Then like a flash in the pan, it was over. One lap around Khufu and a few photos later, our visit to the pyramids was over. Yes, they are fantastic to see and are huge compared to many things you'd see in countless other places. But the actual location is pretty mild and has very little to offer other than those three humps. As incredible and as monstrous as they were, it felt a little underwhelming. I was sadly surprised to find myself not as impressed by them as I thought I would be.

We took a ride to another part of the same area to see all three of the pyramids in the distance. I remember this is where I got a little emotional after Tamara took a photo of me in front of them. I looked at the picture on the camera and got a little choked up. Turning to her, I said, "I've been waiting 30 years for this photo". I remember I actually got her to take the same photo with my phone, and I uploaded it to Facebook with that exact sentence. I wasn't in tears or crying, but I was undoubtedly emotional. I had finally accomplished the one thing on my bucket list that I had thought about for so long. The weight of that accomplishment hit me at that moment. I stood there, enjoyed the view, and knew that if I could do this after so long, I could accomplish anything I set my mind to. Our tour guide took a great photo of Tamara and I together and then off to the Sphinx we went.

Again, another fantastic monument where we took some great photos and absorbed everything we were looking at. Many of the tourists were taking some of the "tacky" forced perspective photos. Pictures that made it look like you were kissing the monument and stuff like that were typical for locals to help you pose for photos. That actually brought us to our first real encounter with the differences between the Egyptian people and Jordanians.

Before departing for Jordan, I had spoken to some colleagues of mine who had taken a similar trip. They commented on how genuinely different these neighbors are. Although the two countries are so close to one another, there was a noticeable cultural difference in how they treat foreigners. One thing we had noticed in Jordan was how friendly, and happy people were. Peddlers in Jordan were generally polite and not pushy or aggressive at all. We experienced a polar opposite of this in Cairo.

In Egypt, particularly near the Sphinx, we had many people harass us to buy things. As we were leaving, one woman, in particular, asked us repeatedly about buying something of hers and kept reducing the price. Despite kindly saying "no thank you" several times, the woman began to follow us and insisting that we purchase something from her. I tried to decline several more times politely as she continued to follow us until, eventually, my response to her became a very stern "NO." I didn't want to become angry or be impolite, but it seemed that in this case, a little more emphasis on the "no" was all that would stop her from continuing to pursue us.

From there, our guide took us to downtown Cairo where we got to see more of the busy city itself. We got to walk across a bridge over the Nile River, wander the streets of old Cairo, and see and experience much of what the few hours we had there could give us.

Just as the tour was getting closer to finishing, we had a minor incident with our tour guide. It felt like a more subdued version of the aggressive peddling of local merchandise. One of the big things with many of these tours in different parts of the world is that the guide usually knows someone at various shops and other locales. They'll take you to these specific locations knowing that you are probably going to buy something there. The guide will get a kickback from the owner for bringing business to his/her shop. We saw this in Jordan and in Israel. Depending on the country and culture, the attitude about it varied.

Our guide had suggested we not buy anything from any of the shops we went into as he assured us he could get us a better deal at a place he knew of. Well, the reality was, we had no idea what his friend's shop would have, and I spotted something in one store that I really wanted, so I bought it. After discovering that I had purchased something, our guide got very upset and stormed outside and insisted that we follow him. Until then, he had been relatively calm and talkative. Now he was quiet and rushing us through the streets until we eventually did get to his friend's shop. Although there were a few items of note in the store, he didn't have anything interesting to me, so I was even happier to have stopped at the previous shop.

Tamara and I sat down with him and had some tea. At this point, our guide seemed to have calmed down. He gave the lowdown on some of the buildings and traditions in the area we were in. We chatted with a few locals, and then before we knew it, we were on our way back to the airport and ready to go to South Africa.

After having waited 30 years to visit this place, Egypt was not at all what I had expected. At that point in my life, I had already experienced some pretty unique places in the world. My visit to Jordan was not that far behind me. It was such an incredible experience that even something like seeing the pyramids wasn't likely to eclipse it. If I had done Egypt before Jordan, I think it may have been a different experience. I would not have had any exposure to anything that ancient before. After seeing Petra and the wonders of Jordan, Egypt almost felt like an afterthought.

A colleague who had seen both commented that seeing the pyramids is quite incredible, but that's it. Once you see them, there's nothing else there to see. Whereas when you go to Petra, it just goes on and on for what seems like forever. I never truly understood what he meant until I experienced it myself, and I do have to agree. I was so happy to cross the pyramids off my list, but they were not as impressive as I had thought they would be. Plus, what you envision as a child is never the same as what you see as an adult. I hope that at some point, I will return to Egypt and do a full tour of all the country has to offer. I am sure that it will allow me to better appreciate the country's unique wonders.

We got back to the airport and made our way to the gate, and before we knew it, we were on our way to South Africa. The only notable thing about that actual flight was how ridiculously hot the plane was. I remember sitting in my seat and wondering if I might actually die from the heat. As the plane climbed higher into the air, the temperature seemed to slide downward. Either that or I was becoming so light-headed that I just didn't notice the heat anymore.

I had scheduled vacation time before my classes in J'Burg. We flew into the city, slept their overnight, and then returned to the airport for a pickup to take us to Klasserie, a part of Kruger National Park. For that one day in the city, we really just wandered around Nelson Mandela Square and a few of the side streets to snap some photos then went to bed.

The next morning, we got up and headed back to the airport.

The poor cab driver really didn't know where he was supposed to drop us off, and it didn't look like anyone was anywhere near where we were supposed to be. He eventually dropped us off, and we waited, and waited, and waited, and wondered if the bus would ever come. Several other people waiting for the same bus made calls, and they kept being told that the bus was on its way. After what felt like a couple of hours of waiting, the bus finally showed up, and we began the journey.

Now to better understand where we were going and how long it took, you may want to punch up a Google map and type in "O.R. Tambo to nThambo" and see the result. You'll quickly realize that it's more than 5 hours from the airport to our final destination. This was going to be a really long bus ride, so for both of us, we really wanted the end result to be worth it.

In retrospect, there's very little about the bus ride I remember beyond just being tired and making the odd pit stop for gas and bathroom breaks. We eventually came to a place called Hoedspruit. Turns out, this is a common stopping point for pretty much every safari bus heading to Kruger. From there, a local driver takes you to whichever campsite you are staying at. This is where things would really start, and we would get a glimpse of how the next four days would play out.

To better get a sense of what it's like to be in the African bush, or at least in that part of Africa, I'll set the stage for you. At that time of year, early-May, it's the dry season. This means that the air and ground itself are pretty dry and, to some extent, feels desert-like. There's no big blue lakes or oceans, just tan colored dirt, and sand that seemed to have sprouted Marula trees, grass, and bushes everywhere. Entire fields of tall yellow and tan grass would appear to be sprinkled in amongst regions of trees and shrubs. As far as the eye can see, there are virtually no large buildings, paved roads, or anything "modern" in appearance. Dirt roads seem to go off into nowhere and then appear near a camp or small structure. Virtually no power lines or poles to be seen everywhere save for the odd one at a campsite. In some parts of the bush, you'd seen entire sections of land surrounded by trees or shrubs that seemed to serve as a natural property line. The trees, roads, shrubs, sand, dirt, and mildly barren landscape seem to go on forever.

In the midst of all of this, you throw in a ton of wildlife. By wildlife, I mean **wild life**. This is not a zoo. This is an open landscape where anything and everything lives, and people are merely *in the way*. Some manmade fences and blockades do prevent some of the animals from wandering into specific areas. Still, by far and large, the animals roam free, so regardless of where you are, you should expect to see something wandering through your path.

Our local guide picked us up and drove us towards the camp, and as we went, we started to spot wildlife on the way there. A couple of giraffes popped up along the side of the road, and we spotted the odd elephant and other small animals as well. At this point, we started to realize exactly where we were and what we were about to experience. Before we knew it, we were at camp sometime around 4pm, and we were some happy to finally be there. We were greeted by a nice young lady named Lily, who offered us some refreshments as we unloaded.

In doing my research for this excursion, I was surprised by the wide variety of accommodations available. From huge luxury hotel-like lodgings to camping in a tent in the middle of the bush, you have many options on where to stay. Cost also played a factor in where we were going to be sleeping. Still, honestly, it didn't matter that much because one way or the other, we wanted to experience wild Africa.

I had come across a place called nThambo Tree Camp. The reviews on Trip Advisor were through the roof, and the price was not bad for all things considered. It's technically considered part of Kruger National Park but more like "greater Kruger" than the central park itself. Klasserie Reserve is a private reserve in the corner of Kruger and looked like the best spot for a couple of folks like us. The more I read about this place, the more I fell in love with the idea of staying there. You mostly sleep in the open, raised tree houses which are right smack in the middle of the bush. There's no fence or protective barrier of any kind around the camp. Animals do come in and out of the area quite frequently. I decided that if we were going to go all this way and see the African bush, why not plunk ourselves down right in the middle of it. Just go for it with nothing holding ourselves back and see what the experience is like. Turns out, it was the best decision we ever made.

The staff and facilities were phenomenal. We had unlimited drinks, three full meals a day, and a fantastic view of the area. Very clean, and best of all, we felt very safe there. Although it is quite open (elephants have been known to walk into camp and drink out of the pool water), you never really felt like you could be in danger. Truthfully, I think the idea of the animals being able to wander around actually added to the allure of the place.

Going out to see the wildlife was what this was all about, so we were excited to go out for the first time that evening. Most safaris follow the same basic idea. You do a run in the morning and one in the late afternoon/early evening. In the middle of the afternoon, most of the animals are off hiding from the heat. We did arrive later in the day but not late enough that we would miss the early evening excursion.

We all piled into a Land Rover, and off we went. Within a matter of minutes, we were spotting elephants along the path and one right in front of us. In fact, there was a baby elephant, and what I presume was its mother on the road directly in our path. We had to stop to wait for it to move out of the way. Our guide instructed us to stay as quiet as possible around the animals to prevent them from getting scared. He actually sits pretty much on the hood of the jeep in a specially rigged chair where he could see clearer. He also had a large shotgun sitting beside him in case things got hairy.

We ended up at a drinking hole where a bunch of the elephants were hanging out. Another baby followed its mother pretty close, and all of the animals were drinking from the little pond. We looked and looked and couldn't spot any hippos in the water until all of a sudden, as if on cue, a big fat nose and two eyes peered out of the water. It was never more than that, but I was glad I had a zoom on my camera as it provided the best shot of a hippo I could have asked for. Driving along the roads and through the bush, it was clear that it would be an exciting few days. Eventually, we headed back to camp, had supper, and then it was time to head to bed.

We had been told that when the time comes for us to go to our treehouses at night, to make sure that one of the guides comes with us to make sure all is clear. As we informed them that we wanted to go to bed, Matt, one of the guides, told us that an elephant had taken a liking to our treehouse. He started to walk us towards it but then instructed us to get into a nearby jeep immediately. We waited for a minute or so, and then he told us the animal had moved and we could go to our bed.

At this point, it's pitch black outside, so we can't really see much, but we make our way up the stairs and are thinking about going to bed. Then we started to hear some noise outside, and we wondered what's going on. I grabbed the flashlight but kept it pointed away from the open spaces. We had been told that day to never shine a flashlight on an elephant at night because it can cause them to have short term blindness and can really scare them. We got out onto the porch and pointed the light away from the sound. A couple of crunching sounds later, we realized the elephant had returned.

We stood on the porch and listened and watched him eat a portion of the tree right beside our cabin. Within a couple of minutes, he wandered off, and we had one hell of a story to finish our first night in South Africa. What would tomorrow bring?

If day one of our trip had a theme, that would have been elephants. Day two's theme would be all about lions. We spent most of the day following and observing a particular pride of lions. It started in the morning, where we spotted a few here and there while out on the jeep. Enoch, our adventurous guide, had Matt the driver take us down into this small canyon, which looked like it may have had water at one time. It seemed very much like Enoch was reading the ground or the air or something in particular. Still, we never really understood what it was he was looking for. It was interesting to see how he would observe the bush and look around us and just somehow know to go in one particular direction or another. We did find a small pride of lions, which we followed for a little while. For us, the real adventure of seeking out lions within the plains would come later in the afternoon.

Later that day, we found ourselves once again feeling like we were driving around aimlessly trying to see animals. At some point, Enoch got out of the jeep and told the driver something, and we left him there. No idea where he was going or how we would find him later, we drove around for what felt like almost an hour before we came back up to meet our guide again. Seems this time, he knew where the more significant pride was, and we were about to be led on quite a little adventure.

Although it was the bush, there were dirt roads and paths everywhere, so it was relatively easy for the jeep to navigate from location to location. For this little excursion, off-roading wouldn't even begin to describe where we went. Enoch led Matt into the bush and guided him in what seemed to be the most illogical route he could have possibly chosen. Many large bushes and trees blocked our paths, and yet the jeep just kept going either over them, through them, or around them.

I cannot stress how odd it was to be plowing through some of this area. Large tree bushes would block the path, and Enoch would insist that we go straight through them with Matt just looking at him with a sense of bewilderment. Several times he'd question where we were going, and Enoch would insist that we keep moving forward. I am sure we drove over large bushes that no vehicle should ever attempt to climb over. It was as if Enoch himself were a lion and was following the scent of his prey. He led the jeep on this daring bushwhacking journey until eventually, he got Matt to slow down. Enoch then turned and told everyone to be extremely quiet and not say a word. No sounds of any kind were to be made, and with that, we knew something was coming up.

The bush completely surrounded us, and so it seemed quite odd that we would ever find anything here. Then, just as the jeep started to reach a little clearing, our intrepid guide remained silent but waved his arm to the right giving us a sign to look. Sure enough, just a few feet from the jeep were an entire family of lions. There were at least two, if not three cubs and several adult female lions just sitting there amongst the tan grass.

As Matt slowly maneuvered the jeep, we got a much better view. There couldn't have been more than 10-20 feet from the vehicle to any of those lions. Every one of the lions literally just sat there and never moved. They looked at us and looked at each other and remained relatively still. As we watched a bit closer, I saw a paw appear as if popping up from the ground. I would never have believed it had someone told me, just as I am telling you, but another cub was lying on his back with his paws up in the air. I remember thinking that it was like looking at my own cat back home who greets me at the door by lying on his back and asking me to rub his belly. The two cats couldn't be more different in size and appearance, but here was proof that they both shared the same genome as my tiny cat back home. I wasn't, however, about to get out and rub this cat's belly.

We must have stayed there for 20 minutes or so. During that time, another tour was out trying to find the lions as well. Matt had radioed to the other jeep about where we were, and sure enough, they showed up in the distance behind us. It was entertaining to see because the vehicle that came in got stuck trying to turn around from where they were. I don't think they were as cautious as our driver and guide were when they came in as it took them quite a while to figure out how to turn around and get out. A lot of comments went back and forth over the radio. Neither Matt nor the driver of the other jeep could understand how we had arrived where we were at. There we were watching in amazement as this pride was just lying there.

Eventually, we did turn the jeep around, taking out a tree or two in the process, and headed back to camp for supper. Of all four days on safari, that one excursion to see that pride of lions stands out as the most memorable and unforgettable part of that trip. By the time we were getting closer to camp, the sun had set, and it was dark, and we spotted more lions on our way back. It was interesting seeing them in the dark but not anywhere near as impressive as seeing them so close to us in the daytime. On that same day, I also experienced something I never thought I would ever do. I put poop in my mouth. Yes, I am serious.

Before we set out on the badass bushwhacking in the park, Enoch took a small group of us on a walk through the bush. He talked a lot about the plants and wildlife and how things survived in the heat. Talked about birds and many of the types of game you'd spot out in the bush while walking. We all stayed behind him as he took us through a path. At some point during the trek, he started talking about a game where folks would try to guess an animal by its droppings. That conversation eventually led to him telling us about some of the species out there and how everything they would eat was vegetable or plant-based. He then proceeded to tell a story about how some of the local kids would pick up some of the round, almost spitball shaped droppings, put them in their mouth and spit them out as far as they could go. Whoever shot the farthest was declared the winner.

He then picked one up, put it in his mouth, and spit it as far as it would go. I couldn't believe what I was seeing. What shocked me even more was when he asked us to try it. Tamara picked one right up and did the same thing. They both urged me to do this, but I said no. There was no way I was putting a piece of crap in my mouth, let alone play a game with it. In the heat of the moment, I found myself not wanting to insult Enoch or the culture he was sharing, so I picked one up, closed my eyes, and popped it in and shot it out as fast as I could. Thankfully, he was right in that there was no flavor whatsoever, and now I could tell this tale to others and never have to do it again.

Our last full day in Africa as tourists had a theme of giraffes. Within 10 minutes of leaving camp in the morning, we saw a couple of fields filled with the tall creatures. Along with a few zebras here and there, it almost felt like a zoo: This was the real thing. We snapped a pile of photos of them and kept on moving.

The rest of the day was a bit of a mish-mash of animal observation. We saw elephants wandering the plains. We saw buffalo and impala. At one point, we just about missed a few rhinos roaming in behind some trees that ran parallel to the road we were on. It was only our guide's keen eye that spotted them as we drove by and then slowed down to get a good glimpse of them. We spotted many different kinds of birds, a chameleon, and even a cool owl just hanging out on a tree. All in all, a pretty good day filled with lots of wildlife but with one major mammal missing from our list: the leopard.

In Africa, the Big 5 refer to lions, elephants, Cape Buffalo, rhinos, and leopards. We had managed to see four of those five animals, and we were on a hunt for the last one. Throughout the safari days, we had been told that the leopard was the hardest one to see. The way it was described to us was essential that you don't get to see the leopard unless the leopard wants to see you. We did have a close call with one near our camp as we were told one was literally wandering around about 100m from our main lodge. Unfortunately, we never did get to see one out in the wild.

Our last safari run was on Sunday, and it would be in the morning before catching the bus to go back to J'Burg. This morning started off really foggy, and while sitting on the jeep, we got a pretty wicked view of the sunrise through the fog. One of my favorite pictures from Africa was taken that morning while out on safari. The theme of that morning would be buffalo as we saw a lot of them. And I do mean *a lot* of buffalo. There were fields and fields filled with them, and they all seemed to be moving together in the same general direction. They are some of the ugliest looking animals to see, but man, they are bigger than you think. Not something I'd want to have to see coming right at me. The whole morning consisted of seeing mostly buffalo along with the odd monkey or bird here and there.

Speaking of monkeys, we did have an exciting monkey

encounter during our stay, but we never did get to see him up close. Our cabins/tree houses were open, which meant that anything could climb in at any time. There were blinds and such you could close when you slept and a door to keep things out. During the day, the windows were open, and so the room itself was free as well. One day after our morning excursion, Tamara found a few crappy presents on the bed. Turns out a monkey or two had gone exploring in our room. We laughed it off and wished we had seen them visit.

After the buffalo excursion, we took some final photos, said our goodbyes, and headed back out on the bus. Much like the trip to the camp, the return was just as uneventful. The only thing I recall now about that trip back was stopping for a meal in a military base of some kind where we had really crappy food. Before we knew it, we were at the airport, catching the Gautrain back into the city and heading back to our hotel, where I'd be staying for the rest of the week. The time I spent in the town was virtually no different than being in any other city I had taught a class in. It almost seemed surreal to have traveled so far, seen so much, to have the latter portion of the trip be so mundane. By the time Saturday came, I was glad to be returning home. The return was just as tiring as the journey to Africa. Still, I was spared the considerable amount of travel woes that my wife experienced as she encountered flight cancellations and delays when she returned. We both made it back in one piece and now had one more fantastic adventure to add to our collection.

My wife recently pointed out something about that trip that I had never considered. Those few days out in the bush were some of the most relaxing vacation days I had ever had. I mean, we literally sat around or slept during the afternoon, and all we ever did when we did go out was sit on a jeep and look at animals. I had never thought about how laid back and relaxing a trip like that actually was.

Africa is definitely its own animal in that it really is not like anywhere else in the world. It can be an expensive place to get to but take my advice and save some money and make the journey there. It's a place you won't soon forget.

Exploring the Rural-Urban Chaos of India

The mere mention of the country of India typically inspires thoughts of many call centers, chaotic streets, and a sense of the disparity between the rich and poor. For most individuals, the only exposure to this country has been through what they see on television or through word of mouth from the odd person they know that have been there. I was no different. Had it not been for my work assignments, India is a country I may never have visited. Thankfully, I am glad I had the chance.

I was sent to India on two separate occasions to teach some classes. This gave me quite a bit of reason to learn at least a bit more about where I was going and what I should expect. As much as you can read about a place, nothing really prepared me for what I would see.

Before I left, I spoke to a couple of colleagues and friends who had been there before. Every single person I talked to shared the same opinion. They all agreed that India was an exciting country to visit and experience the culture and way of life, but it wasn't a place they were eager to return to. Anecdotes aside, their recollections of India all included a similar theme. It was the one site where the culture shock was the most apparent to them. I was told to expect a completely opposite way of life than you've ever seen. In many ways, this was absolutely true.

Now, as a tourist, when you think of India, you think of the Taj Mahal, so I'm in India, and I may never be back, so now is the time to see the Taj. I did my research on TripAdvisor (my preferred travel research website) and found a tour company to get a tour of the Taj. The Taj is about 2.5hrs by car from Delhi in a place called Agra, so I made the reservation and was looking forward to seeing this iconic place. I flew to Delhi from Toronto (14.5 hours), and arrived late at night, so I checked into my hotel, slept, then got up in the morning. I was met by my tour guide, who was my sole companion, as we drove towards Agra.

I have often commented that I have always wanted to visit a place where it almost felt like an alien world. I've always wanted to experience situations where the culture and people were so utterly different than I am used to. And as we turned onto a side road on our approach to Agra, I would get my chance to experience a culture reasonably different than my own.

The first thing I started to notice was how most of the buildings and homes were in serious disrepair. Buildings in shambles, blocks of concrete lying about from construction that was apparently abandoned, and shacks made of corrugated metal littered the sides of the roadway. Little shops set up every so often where collections of locals seemed to be conjugating and staring at any cars that drove by. People looked no different than anyone I had seen before, but yet somehow, it just felt foreign to me.

The driver then spoke up and told me about the cattle and monkeys. In India, cows are considered sacred and, therefore, never eaten or slaughtered. He pointed a few of them out along the side of the road. That didn't seem to be a big deal at first. But these were among the buildings, the people, and even the streets itself. It was uncanny to see a cow or two just wandering the streets like we'd see a dog or cat. Unlike back home, however, no one honks their horn at the cow or makes any sort of action to move them out of the way. If the cow decided to sit in the middle of the road, everyone would drive around it. Wild monkeys, goats, cats, and dogs alike were also visible as we went through this main street towards our destination.

I kept flipping my perspective from one side of the car to the other to try and take in as much as I could. In some cases, the stores look just like any other shop you'd see in your own town or in the movies. Then we'd drive by stores where the building seemed solid, but inside it was just stacks of tires, or have broken down pieces of machinery, and then beside it, you'd find a shop selling cell phones and data plans.

I started to be reminded of my time in Jordan and how the

streets of Madaba were so dirty and filled with garbage that for a moment, I thought I was somewhere else. The streets were littered with the rubble of buildings and rotting food about. In some spots, it felt very much like I was driving through a giant garbage heap with people weaving in and out of it like it was commonplace.

For another "blink and you'll miss it" moment, I spotted a man with his back to me and a small stream of fluid shooting out from in front of him. As a guy, it was clear as day to me that he had answered the call of nature right there in the street as if it were the usual place to go. As it would turn out, this would be the first of many, many times I would spot someone going number one along the road or.

Upon arrival into downtown Agra, we stopped, and my guide got in, introduced himself, and gave me the rundown on where we were going. I told him I needed to use an ATM to get some cash, which became our first stop. I took out 4000 rupees, which is roughly about 80 Canadian dollars. It felt bizarre to be carrying bills that were marked as 1,000. Still, I knew I'd eventually need the money for attractions, tips, or keepsakes. A quick pop back in the car, we drove another 5 minutes and out we were on our way to the Taj.

We arrived at a time when crowds were low, as it was still early in the morning. The first thing I had to do was get in line to go through security and then get a ticket for entrance into the facility. I would find out later that locals apparently get in for extremely cheap while the tourists get reamed for their cash. 1,000 rupees for my ticket vs. the 10 my guide had to pay. I didn't care how much it was as I knew I wanted to go. When I converted the money to Canadian, it was about $20, and to me, that was still a fair price to see such a great attraction.

Security was unusual in that they were adamant that no electronics were permitted. Still, cameras were allowed, and no one ever said anything about my GPS. This was the same GPS that I had brought to Petra in Jordan.

We came in through the West gate for which my guide told me was less common for tourists and far more common for locals. Walking east, he started pointing out various parts of the area, and we hadn't even got to the main entrance yet.

Then we turned left and headed into the Great Gate, where the Taj itself became visible. My guide started on a spiel about how symmetry was a massive thing for the construction of this place. He stood me in one specific spot and told me to look at the Taj itself. From that exact location, everything on one side looked precisely the same as the other. Exact and perfect symmetry was clearly visible from this spot. The moment I moved one tile ahead or back, the image was different. Although it was a small thing to do, it clearly showed how much time and effort had been put into keeping things balanced. As someone who likes to think of balance as ruling my life, it was fantastic to see this being played out in the real world. The theme of symmetry would follow the rest of my Taj visit. My guide would point out how different buildings were created exclusively to keep the grounds symmetrical. An entire building on one side of the Taj was built solely because a building was present on the other side.

After you exit the gate, you enter a garden. This is a long stretch of water between the Great Gate and the Taj itself. We walked along the walkway, snapped some photos, and then made our way to the main attraction. As we got closer, I slipped on a pair of shoe covers to prevent myself from leaving any shoe marks on any part of the actual monument. Once inside, you could get a real good look at the fantastic intricate art that had been applied to the building. It was clear as day that marble and gemstones lined the walls. The intricacy and detail of the work were astounding. Parts of the gems themselves would absorb light while others would reflect it. The entire thing was built as a tomb, and every day thousands flock to it to admire the theatrical nature of its beauty. We did a walk around and then eventually headed back towards the garden, and ultimately left the place entirely.

The next stop on my tour of the day was the Agra Fort. In doing research for my vacation time in India, pretty much every article that came up said that if you were doing the Taj, you should do the fort. I had never heard of the fort and didn't know anything about it, but since it was part of the tour, why not go?

My guide's knowledge of the history of the building and its surroundings was quite impressive. He told me a whole lot of stories about the place. Still, I was more focused on seeing the building and grounds area itself instead of hearing the story. Part of me wants to feel guilty for not listening as carefully as I could about the history. For me, it's all about observations of the places I go to and less about the historical significance.

As we left, a couple of wild monkeys were sitting at the main gate just off to the side. My expertise in simian species is less than none, so I couldn't tell you what kind they were. I do recall them watching all the tourists coming in and out of the fort. Surprisingly, they resembled a couple of homeless people looking for handouts. I smiled and was reminded of the two homeless guys from "Coming to America" and wondered if the monkeys had seen the movie.

Following my time at the fort, the driver took me directly to a restaurant called Indiana, which was somewhat of a surprising name given where I was. I told the waiter that I didn't really know the food, so he was quite accommodating and explained what they had and what was most popular. I ordered a Kabab, and although I didn't partake in any local sauces, the food itself was quite tasty, albeit a bit spicy for me. I kept a business card from the restaurant and pinned it to my cubicle back at work.

After lunch, it became clearer what my tour guide's true intentions were for me. Sure, I was being shown the sights and sounds of Agra but there was more to it apparently. For every stop we made, there was a push to purchase something from whatever location we happened to visit.

One store along the tour was where marble is carved for decorative purposes. They showed the entire process of how they cut the marble and insert the jewels into the sculpture. The method used by these same people was used to carve and decorate the walls of the Taj. At first, it seemed really nice, but after seeing how it's all done, the hard sell starts. The guy working there kept going on about how sales of their merchandise are used to help the local economy and that it's a dying art. He tried over and over again to get me to buy some big-ticket items. Now, as beautiful as they all were, there wasn't anything that really stood out for me as being affordable and exciting enough to take home. We're talking $85 for a tiny little "box" (fit in the palm of my hand) that I ended up buying just to get something from India. As I would find out later, I got hosed royally. Yes, sure, it's made locally and uses the same techniques as their ancestors did, but it certainly was not worth what I paid.

The next place they took me to was a place where they make rugs by hand. They actually had two guys at the front of the store who were weaving the rugs. The work itself was amazingly well crafted by these workers who literally spun cloth while singing to keep a rhythm going as they worked. Much like the marble shop, the owner was all about trying to sell me rugs. Now, these aren't rugs you buy at your local Walmart. These were all priced at several hundred dollars or more. The owner repeatedly tried to push me into buying a rug. I explained several times that although they were beautiful, it wasn't something I wanted. It got to be a bit uncomfortable when he kept asking, and I just kept telling him no. He finally took me into a spot where they had scarves that had been made. Despite the crazy price, I did opt to get one for Tamara as she wears these, and I wanted to give her something from India. It was definitely more than I would typically pay for a scarf. Still, it did pay off because when she got it for Christmas, she loved it and wore it almost every day for weeks.

After having been to two of these so-called "stops" on my tour, I was becoming annoyed by the fact that the trip had become more about trying to sell me stuff than to show me the sights. Each time I came out of one of these places, the "guide" asked me if I had bought anything. For the first two shops, I told him I had made a small purchase. As we continued, the pressure to make larger purchases was increasing. It was clear the guide was trying to make a buck off kickbacks by parading me through these local stores. I asked if we could go some where I could get some simple souvenirs, and he said it was coming, but next, we had to go see some jewelry.

The shop was more like a museum than a store. The jewelry there was gorgeous, but this was definitely way out of my league. As a person, I'm about as down to earth as it gets. I wear t-shirts, jeans, and a ball cap. I don't do suits and avoid dressing up as much as possible, as it just doesn't fit my personality. I don't live check to check, but I have debt just like everyone else. What I am not is someone who shops at Tiffany's or Gucci and wears $500 jeans and over-priced "fashionable" clothing and drives a Bentley. The moment I walked into the "shop" part of this museum, I knew it was not a place for me. Sure, I'd love to buy my wife a beautiful fancy ring or necklace, but I wasn't about to cough up, nor could I afford anything in this store. I felt like I had somehow stumbled upon the Indian version of Cartier or Harry Winston. This was not the kind of store I belonged in.

I looked around through the glass display cases and smiled and then proceeded to turn around and leave. I was done. I had had enough of being handed from shop to shop to try and extort money out of me. My tour guide immediately asked me why I didn't buy anything, and I told him I wasn't interested. He was visibly annoyed and then asked if I wanted to go to another place with keychains and other stuff I might be interested in. Nope, I was done, so I told him I was ready to go back to Delhi. Having spent the latter part of the day listening to hard-sell pitches from people peddling their wares, I'd had enough.

Before my trip, one of the warnings I had read was about the hard sell, but I was not prepared for how hard it really is. Should you choose to visit India, be ready for this kind of treatment. Perhaps make it known ahead of time that you aren't interested in making purchases but just want to see the sights. Despite that, I would definitely recommend a visit to Agra if you have the chance to go.

After returning to the hotel, I went for a walk around and was quite surprised that even a mall in India is the same as it is back home. No matter where you go, malls are still filled with 80% clothing shops that all sell the same stuff. The best part, however, was seeing a McDonald's with no Big Mac or other beef "burgers" on the menu. Instead of a Big Mac, it's a Chicken Maharaja Mac. It looks like a Big Mac but has chicken instead of beef and uses habanero sauce and jalapenos with shredded onions. At one other location, I actually tried the Indian version of KFC, which was far too hot for my taste.

The next morning, I got up and checked out of my hotel and waited for my driver to take me to the airport. My employer had insisted that for security and safety reasons, I should pre-book a driver through my company before my arrival. They had indicated that cabs may not be as reliable. However, that morning I experienced my second issue with the company providing my transportation during this trip.

After explaining to the concierge who I was waiting for, he called my driver. We came to discover that my driver had arbitrarily decided to skip picking me up. The hotel quickly got me a different driver, and I was on my way to the airport. In no time flat, I was back on a plane and heading for Bangalore. I landed and had no issues finding my driver this time, and after about a 45-minute drive, I got to my hotel and was glad to be there. Unpacked, had a shower, watched some TV, and then crashed. My real adventure in Bangalore was to begin the next day.

My first day was both exciting and terrifying, all at once. It started just fine with the car service picking me up at the hotel and taking me to work, and that drive to work was one of the most interesting I had had yet. Because of where the hotel was located, we had to take this weird rotten road that ran along the edge of a military base. The street is mostly a dirt road intermixed with pavement here and there, and in some cases, you would assume it was one way, but that's not how they roll here. Between the cows, goats, and dogs and people walking in and out of traffic, it was pure chaos on the drive into the office, and I loved every minute of it. It was just such a departure from what I was used to that I just reveled in how different things really were. On my way to work each day, I would tweet out how many cows or other animals had blocked our passage to the office.

I spent the day teaching a class, and although there were a few cultural differences, the guys there were really good to deal with. However, at the end of that workday, I had what I would consider to be the scariest moment I've ever had in all of my travels.

This was the third and final strike against the car service. I had my confirmation for a pickup that day at my office for 4:30pm. I had the driver's phone number, car model, and license plate information. 4:45 came and no car. 5pm came, and no car and I finally tried to call him. I had been told that the car service had "good English speaking drivers." This guy couldn't understand much of what I was saying and proceeded to say something about being at "the gate."

The office is in a secured area, so cars have to pass through a gate. I thought maybe the driver meant he was there and couldn't get through. I walked up to the entrance but no sign of his car. Auto rickshaw and other vehicles were everywhere to be seen. Random people were walking on the sidewalk and on the road. A handful of cows played out their own version of Frogger by weaving in and out of traffic at rush-hour. I spotted a couple of stray dogs humping each other right there in the median between both lanes which gave me a momentary laugh before the apprehension returned. It was massive congestion of anything and everything in one place. Looking out into this bubble of activity, none of those cars had my name on it.

I went back into the office and asked one receptionist where car services are supposed to pick us up, and she had no idea. I asked another person if she could call the guy on the phone, and she did. Turns out, he was on the other side of town. For some reason, he thought our office was somewhere else, so there was no way this guy was going to pick me up. I was told to find another way back.

At this point, it's pushing 5:15pm, and I'm starting to wonder exactly how I am getting back to my hotel.

The hotel! They have car services. I called the hotel, and the woman on the phone was accommodating. She said she'd call me back with information on car availability. I took a deep breath and felt better. The sound of "Take a Picture" by Filter came on my phone, and sure enough, the hotel had called back. No cars were available until 8pm. Uh oh.

At this point, I'm getting a little freaked out. It's pushing towards 5:30, and I knew I couldn't walk back because it's well over an hour away on foot. I'm in the middle of a city I don't know, with massive chaos on the streets. No taxis in sight and only a small, limited amount of cash on me, I go back out to the gates and look around, and then it hits me, "WTF am I going to do?"

I don't know a soul in the office here. I don't speak the language, and I don't know the area at all. Cars and livestock are wandering everywhere with hundreds of horns blasting each other, trying to drive through what seems to be the most chaotic system of roads I've ever seen. And on top of all that, it's 32° C outside, and I am already sweating from the heat alone.

I then started to get really freaked out. As I am sure some of you know, when your mind begins to panic, rational thought goes right out the window. Yes, I probably could have gotten in one of those rickshaws and found my way back to the hotel. I could have possibly gone back inside the office and see if they could call a taxi for me. It's easy to think of these things now after I'm back in a comfortable room feeling a lot calmer about the situation. But at the time, I'm looking around me, and all I am seeing is just chaos everywhere and no way to get out of it. I can feel my heart beating a bit faster, and I know it could get worse.

I stood at the gate entrance to my office, staring out into the streets of Bangalore, utterly clueless as to how I was going to proceed. I'm sure the locals were looking at me and wondering what the silly American was doing (as I am sure they assumed I was from the US). I just stood there almost frozen in time. I then recalled a conversation about my job with my wife's cousin. She once told me she wouldn't be comfortable trying to find her way from one place to another in a strange city like I do all the time. I thought about all the places I had been and all of the things I had experienced and wondered exactly how it was I was going to get back to the hotel.

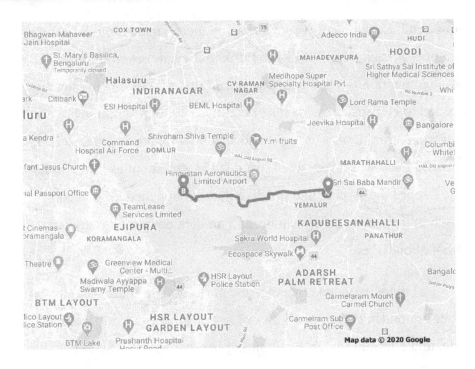

I cannot emphasize how intimidating it was for me at that moment. I paced in front of that gate and just could not think straight about how I would solve this problem. As each moment passed, I could feel myself shaking, my heart throbbing, and the sweat pouring down my face as I became more and more panicked. I'm already hot from the heat and from carrying my laptop backpack on my back. Still, now I'm sweating from panic as I start recalling stories about people getting lost in countries like this. One of my colleagues got stranded in the middle of Noida, India, because of an argument with the driver. The dread of the situation completely blinded me to any rational thought. Every single dreadful scenario of what could happen was playing out in my head. ***What was I going to do?***

Have you seen the movie Inside Out? It's a Pixar movie about how your emotions are actually little creatures that live inside your head. Each one of them works together to make you the whole person you really are. I'd like to think that whatever emotion was paying attention to my situation realized that a switch in my head needed to be flipped on for me to continue. Let's just call her Aurora. Aurora took a moment and saw how freaked out I was and realized there was an answer I just needed a moment to figure it out. She flipped the switch, and just like that, it happened. I glanced down at the screen on my phone, and an idea popped into my head. What about Uber?

I quickly opened the app, and sure enough, there were many Uber options in Bangalore. I picked my destination, said I needed a ride, and 5 minutes later, I was sitting in a car on my way to the hotel. He didn't speak English either, but he had Google Maps on his phone with my hotel dialed in. I breathed a sigh of relief and watched the madness around me continue. He pulled up to the hotel, and I thanked him, feeling a huge sigh of relief.

I can honestly say that for me, at that moment, Uber saved me. Had I not been able to open up my phone and just summon a ride like that without worry, I do not know what I would have done. I was so stricken with panic at the time that nothing else came to mind. I would like to think that I would have eventually calmed down and thought it out rationally. Although when you're scared or freaked out like that, it's hard to think sensibly at all.

I got out of the car, came into the hotel, and it hit me. The brutal wave of emotional panic that was bundled up inside of me burst out in the form of tears as I walked down the hall towards my room. I did my best to conceal it and not be so loud, but I was a nervous wreck. Safe inside the hotel, but just finally realizing how scared I was, I tried my best to get to my room as fast as possible before I lost it.

As I walked down the hall, an employee saw how distressed I was and helped me to my room, put the Do Not Disturb sign on the door for me, and wished me the best. Five minutes later, the assistant manager showed up and wanted to know if I was ok and whether he or the hotel could do anything for me. By then, I had calmed down, but it was such a touching moment to have a complete stranger genuinely concerned for my well-being. It was at that moment that I realized that despite all the flack people give those from India, they really are amazingly friendly and caring. I have a completely different view of their culture, having experienced my time there.

I called my wife, told her the story, and she asked me if I was going to come home early. After sitting in my room long enough, I had come to realize that it was purely my own fears and uncertainties that had made the situation worse. It's tough to remain calm when you start to let your nerves get to you. I told her I would be ok and that I was sure the rest of the week would be better. I was right.

The rest of my stay in Bangalore was actually quite enjoyable. I took another Uber ride out one night to a mall and did a little geocaching. It was certainly interesting being in the middle of Bangalore at night with all of those people and traffic around. I also had one night where the driver who took me back to the hotel made a detour for me and took me to a wicked temple of Ganesh and a great spot for picking up some souvenirs. The hotel was located in a business district, so I didn't get as much of a chance to go exploring on foot. My visit to Mumbai several months later would address that.

No trip to India would be complete without a story about the food. India is quite known for its culinary delights, both spicy and mild. As someone who wasn't a fan of Indian food back home, it was a concern I had when spending any amount of time there. Between the hotel's selections and some of the items at the cafeteria, I did pretty well to stick to the mild side of the palette with one notable exception.

I had taken a liking to this one dish from the cafeteria, which my students called "Indian Chinese food." The mixture of chicken and vegetables was just to my liking. However, the first time I tried it, I encountered the single most memorable food experience of that trip, possibly my life. I was eating the dish and spotted what I believed to be a green bean in amongst the vegetables. I popped the whole thing in my mouth, chewed down and swallowed like it was nothing. Within a mere few moments, I realized this was no green bean. It was a green chili. My mouth flared up, my face turned red, and the sweat began to pour off my forehead and out of my eyeballs. My students started to chuckle as I was panicking for water. I gulped down what I am sure felt like two liters of water as I tried to counter the intensity of the chilies. As the guys at the table laughed, they said I should make sure to have milk with my food to avoid that, or simply not eat the chilies. I followed their advice on the subsequent days. Still, that first day certainly made for a memorable meal and reinforced that Indian food burns going down. Several hours later, I also learned that it burns coming out.

On my last day in Bangalore, I got up bright and early and went for a walk through Commercial Street. This area is well known in the city for its many shops and outdoor shopping areas. I spent a good couple of hours just walking around, getting a sense of what it was like. At first, it felt very much like Chinatown in NYC. Lots of shops in confined spaces but not a lot of good deals. That was until I wandered a bit further. As I got further west from the main Commercial Street area, the shops began to look less and less like NYC's Chinatown and more like something I had seen on TV. Dead chickens were hanging in storefronts. Large boxes of junk sitting on the street and the smell of manure and livestock became more and more prominent the further I got from where I had started. I picked up a small set of earrings for my wife as another souvenir. I would get another chance to do some shopping in the middle of India during a follow-up trip to Mumbai the year after.

After wandering for long enough, I hailed myself a rickshaw drive back to the mall area then snagged an Uber back to the hotel. I was ready to go. I checked out and headed to the airport, but not without one last-ditch effort by the driver to get me to go shopping with him. He really insisted on me taking him shopping in an area so he could get some free shirts for his kids. I told him to take me to the airport and that I was not buying anything else.

I grabbed some food and a few Christmas presents at the airport, got on my plane, and came home. I shared my stories of what India was like with my friends and family and assumed that it was unlikely for me to be returning there anytime soon. Within 6 months, I would end up back there in Mumbai, experiencing something completely different.

While in Mumbai, I stayed at a hotel right in the middle of the city, which allowed me to really go exploring. Each night I would go out and wander around the neighborhood, or take an Uber to another part of the city. On one excursion, I walked from the hotel to a mall, located about 30 minutes from my hotel. Just as I was getting used to weaving in and out of traffic, I got clipped by a motorcycle. My right side was sore for a couple of days. I walked along the Currey Rd Bridge heading towards High Street Phoenix. Google Maps took me on a little detour along a road it listed as "Sitaram Jadhav Marg." This road can be best described as one long stretch of tiny shops on either side. Little shacks filled with many local foods, crafts, and artistry were all you could see from one end of the street to the other.

I also had a chance to walk along the water and see a beautiful sunset over the Arabian Sea. I walked down the street from my hotel and found another back-alley outdoor market filled with many food and craft items unique to the country. I picked up a selection of "hot sauces" for my father-in-law, where the only criteria I had was that it had to have a label on it that I couldn't read. I also had the chance to visit the Gateway to India, a pretty famous and remarkable archway found in downtown Mumbai.

On my final day there, I wandered another part of the city where I got to do a mini-tour of a Masonic temple. I met their secretary and got to see how their temple was decorated and arranged versus the one I attend back home. Like Bangalore, after a while, I was ready to pack up and come home to the more familiar.

In total, I spent about two weeks in India and experienced three distinctly different cities. Agra was a bustling town centered on the Taj Mahal. Bangalore was a friendly, busy city where tourists were few and far between, making it far more welcoming than other places in India. And Mumbai was the largest city in India and provided me a more metropolitan point of view of the country.

My biggest takeaway from India is that it is a country that stands apart from other places I have visited thus far. The disparity of the poor and rich is visible everywhere and, in some cases, will make you realize how fortunate people born in North America really are. Despite my displeasures with the many attempts by locals to get me to spend money, the people in India were amazingly friendly. From hotel staff to my students to my drivers, none of them hesitated to strike up a conversation. I even met a complete stranger on the street who just wanted to talk to me because he could tell I wasn't from the area.

It made me realize that the discomfort I felt while wandering around the streets of India came not from the actual fear of the locals. It was rooted in complete and total ignorance of the people and their culture. Before visiting India, I had only seen it on TV and heard things through people I knew. I never took any time to learn more about them as a people and therefore arrived in that country with a preconceived notion that I, as a foreigner there, would be unsafe. The reality was quite different. I was no safer there than I was in any other city I had visited previously. All the press and propaganda you hear and see gives you a faulty perception of a place, and it sticks with you. This was very similar to how I felt uncomfortable during the first day of my visit to Jordan. Now when I speak of India, I tell stories about what I saw, what I experienced, and how the people were fantastic.

Will I return to India? At one time I would have said no. Still, now I think it's a country that, given the right situation, I would return to explore more of and see what else it has to offer. I will definitely avoid the green chilies next time.

Life & Death in the Pacific Ocean

I don't recall when I first heard about the Galapagos Islands. What I do remember was, at some point in my childhood, I saw photos of the monster-sized "turtles" and couldn't for the life of me imagine how they ever got to be that big. I never forgot the name of the place where they came from, and so I tucked it away and hoped that at some point down the road, I'd get a chance to visit these mystical islands.

Many years later, through the wonders of Facebook, I would reconnect with an uncle I hadn't spoken to in a couple of decades. During one day, I spotted an off-handed comment or status update of some kind from him, which mentioned the Galapagos Islands. I hadn't thought about that place in years, and so a quick web search later, I was reminded again about why I wanted to visit. Through the wonders of frequent flier miles and discounted G Adventures tours, I booked myself a 4-day cruise of the islands, and before I knew it, I was on my way.

I flew out of Halifax, NS, on a United Airlines flight. That was supposed to take me into the US and then onto Ecuador via a connection in Texas. After boarding the plane and seeing ground staff go to and from the cockpit several times, I knew something was up. Usually, they bring the baggage manifest to the captain and then close the door. This time it was in and out several times with the captain leaving once or twice as well. Eventually, he came on to tell us that the flight would be canceled due to a mechanical failure. I've had flights canceled before but rarely during a vacation, so I wasn't a happy camper. To add insult to injury, the "failure" was literally that a knob on his control panel would not turn. That was it. Since the knob couldn't turn, the flight couldn't leave. It was incredibly frustrating, but there was nothing I could do, so I worked with the airline to get me on a new set of flights.

Getting as far as Houston that day, I ended up spending the night in an airport hotel that the airline paid for when I couldn't make my connection to Ecuador. I got up the following morning and took a flight to Panama City, which was then connected to Quito, Ecuador. Although I had missed my tour orientation meeting that afternoon, the departure for the islands was the next day. So, I slept in my room and got up bright and early for yet another flight.

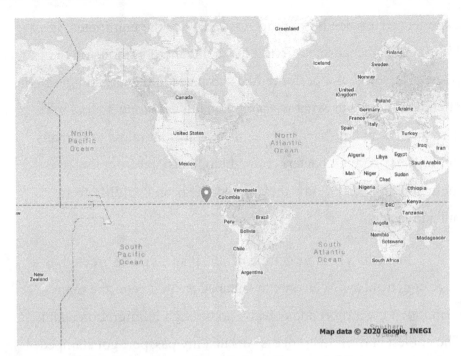

Map data © 2020 Google, INEGI

Depending on your knowledge of geography, you may not realize how far Quito is from Galapagos. For that matter, you may not even know where Ecuador is. Take a quick peek at a Google Map of the Americas. Draw a straight line from the tip of Florida going south (downwards) and pass right over Panama, Ecuador, and then Quito in Ecuador is right there. Once you hit Quito, take your finger and head west (to the left) about 1400kms or roughly 900 miles. That collection of islands is where I was heading.

The tour included an actual flight from Quito to Baltra, where we would catch a bus to take us on the first part of our trip. The flight itself was not all that interesting until we landed. I didn't know it at the time, but many airlines will spray the interior upon landing. This is common for flights from the mainland to various islands around the world. I had heard of this before from a colleague who experienced it when he went to Australia. For the uninitiated, it's a bit unsettling because, at first, it looks like there's smoke on the plane. The smell of a perfume-like substance in the air, and the flight attendants telling us what was going on put everyone's mind to rest. The spray is an anti-bacterial chemical that is harmless to humans but kills any foreign bacteria brought to the island from the mainland. It's part of how they protect the island wildlife from outside factors.

Immediately after getting off the plane, you're greeted by a huge sign that says Welcome to Galapagos. You enter the main terminal of the airport and actually go through immigration again. The coolest part of this process was that my passport got stamped, and the stamp itself was an actual tortoise. It's probably my favorite passport stamp of all the places I have been to thus far.

We all piled onto a bus which took us to a dock where we got on a boat and then got on another bus. The entire time we were traveling, I kept thinking that there was nothing around that jumped out at me as being all that unusual. Again, like other places I have visited, somehow I thought it would be more mystical than it was. I did, however, notice how blue the water was, and how lush and green the grass seemed to be. It was quite beautiful to see.

While on the second bus, our tour guide began to tell us that the first thing we were going to go see was the giant tortoises. This came as a surprise to me. I had expected to see these creatures far later in the tour, if not near the end. A lot of the typical "tour" stuff has the big-ticket items at the end so that they can show you a bunch of other things you're not really all that interested in, which "builds the suspense." Not in this case. We had only been on the island for maybe an hour or so, but we were already being taken to the most significant attraction the islands are known for. To me, this set the stage for what would become a very memorable trip. What a great way to get the visitors excited than to give them exactly what they came for right away. Everything after that would just be a bonus.

We got to the tortoise sanctuary, which was on private property, and the guide gave us a little history. The owner had purchased the property for farming but couldn't keep the tortoises out of his crops. No matter how hard he tried, they kept eating and destroying everything he was trying to grow and farm. Eventually, he decided to switch from farming to tourism and allowed people to visit the tortoises on his property. That ultimately proved to be the more profitable endeavor as he's remained in the tourism business ever since.

The actual area where we got off the bus and began exploring was not all that remarkable. Beyond a gift shop and a few other small buildings, you'd never think of this place as being the home to some of the most amazing animals you could set your eyes on. It was only within a few moments of wandering past the gift shop onto the trail that our guide spotted a "young" tortoise. We heard young and thought small, but this was far from a tiny turtle you might see in someone's aquarium.

Most people, when they hear the word tortoise, they think it's just a giant turtle. To the eyes, that's what they look like, but there is a distinction between tortoises and turtles. Turtles go in the water, but tortoises do not. From what I know, tortoises tend to be bigger but not necessarily the giant size the Galapagos ones are known for. Upon approaching the tortoise for the first time, I found my mind full of contradictions about what I saw. They are much larger than you might think. This first one, which our guide called a "young pup," was still quite significant. Probably about a couple of feet tall and maybe three feet long, it just crept along the forest floor. When you see an animal that size, there is a certain amount of intimidation because, for most of us, we're used to animals of that size being able to jump or attack you. Since tortoises are by their very nature, slow, there's actually nothing to be afraid of.

For me, it took a few minutes for this to sink in as I was watching others get insanely close for photographs, and I kept thinking to myself, "they shouldn't get so close. It might attack them." I would then realize how ridiculous that sounded, but it was just my natural instinct to think like this. Once I really thought about how there was really no danger, I closed in for some fantastic photos.

As we continued our walk through the jungle area, we came upon a massive tortoise. Our tour guide indicated he was at least 100 years old. He must have been perhaps four to five feet long, maybe a bit more, and maybe about 28 inches high. He too moved very slowly but was terrific to see given his size.

Words really cannot describe how hypnotic these animals are. They move at such a slow pace, but you find yourself completely enthralled and captivated by their movements. You stand there and just watch as they make each step seem like a huge hurdle for them to overcome. Again, because they are so slow, capturing great photos with them was really easy.

As we progressed through the woods, our guide pointed out many of the various plant life indigenous to the region. He showcased other places the tortoises might live, eat, and sleep in. He capped the tour off with us back at the gift shop where I picked up a t-shirt and a couple of small souvenirs for home.

I was already overwhelmed by what I had just experienced and was really excited to see what else would come during this trip. We packed up into the bus and headed to the dock. We got on our boat, where we would continue for the remainder of the journey. The ship housed a couple dozen passengers plus the crew in amongst the three decks. The rooms themselves were relatively small, and for most of the passengers, you were doubled up with someone else. For whatever reason, somehow, I ended up with my own room, which was just fine by me.

As we set out on the water towards Floreana, we would sleep through the night as the boat made its way there. Evenings and nights were filled with conversations with other passengers and laying out on the top deck, looking at the stars. With no one else around, and the ocean as big as it is, it really was like being in the middle of nowhere.

Of all wildlife experiences I have had in my life, the second day of my tour of the Galapagos is hands down the most memorable. The day started with a trip to Post Office Bay on the island of Floreana. It gets its name from the famous "post office" located on the northern part of the island. It was a mail relay station used by the visitors to send mail worldwide. In the early days, visitors to the island would leave letters or postcards in the mailbox. The next visitor would go through and find something destined to go to where they were returning to. Now it gets used by tourists to do something similar. I actually sent myself a letter to see if it would come back. Luckily enough, within a couple weeks of my return home, my message would arrive.

Each time they would take us on an outing to a particular island, the pattern was the same. The ship would stop several hundred meters from shore and drop anchor. They would then pile all of us into the dingy boats and bring us directly to shore. There we would spend a couple of hours or so exploring the area. In some cases, it was just walking the trails, and in others, it was snorkeling or swimming. It really depended on the specific island we were visiting. In this case, the post office was the most famous landmark on the island with a small lava tube not far from there as a runner up. I opted to skip the lava tube as I had already made plans for something specific at the post office.

Before my arrival, I looked into doing some geocaching in

the area. I wanted to get at least one geocache while in Ecuador, and there was one located at the mailbox, but it had been marked as missing. I corresponded with the owner and made arrangements to replace the cache there. I did look around several times to try and find the original but came up empty. I also wanted to make sure that no one else saw me actually hide the geocache. The last thing I wanted to do was to get into a long-winded conversation about geocaching. I had the container in my pocket but had to wait as others looked around, and then eventually, I was alone. I found a spot just off to the right of the post office, hid the container, and concealed it well, then made my way back to the beach.

The other item that caught my attention on this island and some of the others was the bright red-colored crabs that littered the rocks. Galapagos is an archipelago formed by ancient volcanic rock; many ancient lava formations encase many beach areas. Hawaii is another such place that is very familiar to many but far more north in the Pacific than the Galapagos. The rocks that formed the bay around the beach were covered with these bright red and orange crabs, which I found fascinating. They were not all that big in the sense that some were large but not thick. I was used to seeing the crabs back home in the Atlantic, where people have them for dinner. Although these guys were bright-colored, there really wasn't much to them.

Similar to Africa, excursions on the boat took place twice a day. We'd go out in the morning, come back for lunch and a siesta, and then head out later in the day. After our post office visit, we headed back to the boat for a little nap. I enjoyed another wildlife experience while sitting on the upper deck.

The top deck of the boat was entirely open to the ocean air. Chairs and loungers were placed all along the edges of the floor, and many people would sit back and enjoy the sun or just take a nap in the sea air. During the break between islands, several of us were gathered on the front side of the deck, chatting away when someone spotted something splashing off to the side. We all looked, and sure enough, a dolphin jumped out of the water beside the boat. Then one of the other passengers called to us to get us to the very front of the ship. Directly in front of the vessel were two or three dolphins swimming. We could see them jumping in and out of the water as they continued along their way. It was almost like they were playing in the water with the boat.

I didn't have my camera, so I just watched as this small pod of dolphins continued to play with the boat almost as if we were chasing them. Then as quickly as it began, the show was over, and the dolphins veered to one side, and we continued along our way.

During the latter part of the day, our guide took us to a charming beach where my favorite memory of the islands took place. He proceeded to tell us a story about sea turtles and how the adults would come to that beach, lay their eggs, and bury them. When they hatch, the sea turtles would have to run as fast as possible to the ocean before being picked off by birds. Most of the turtles wouldn't make it, but the few who did hit water had a better chance of survival.

As he tells this story, I was reminded of the late Steve Irwin and an episode of his television program, "The Crocodile Hunter." He laid on the beach with his arms crossed as one of these baby sea turtles wander across the sand. The camera was zoomed in to his face with a sea turtle walking from left to right and Steve with his giant grin just smiling as he tells the viewer about these cute little animals. I remember him telling the same story as my guide about how many turtles don't survive. He'd also make mention of the fact that it was imperative to leave the turtles alone. They had to fight their own way to the water as this is how nature had intended it.

Our guide pointed to the sky and noted that several birds were circling the beach, and almost as if on cue, one or two people spotted a baby turtle running along the beach. Then just like that, the beach was covered with all of these tiny little sea turtles fleeing towards the water. Having hatched just moments ago, we stood there and witnessed nature in its most beautiful moment. The birds dove down and snatched a few turtles here and there as we yelled at them to stay away. Our guide was quite clear that we were not to interfere with the turtles or attack the birds. One woman was screaming and shaking sticks at the birds and really making quite a scene, but she never laid hands on an animal. I remember clearly seeing so many of these little turtles running to the water. Their short front legs were almost flapping as they were literally hurtling themselves as fast as they could towards the sea.

There had been a bit of rain sprinkling on and off that evening. I had been hesitant to take out my camera for too long for fear of it getting wet. But standing on that beach, watching these little turtles run for their life, I knew this was a once in a lifetime opportunity. I dug out my camera, and I took as many photos and videos as I could. It seemed that the more turtles appeared, the harder the rain came down. I put the camera into video mode and focused all my attention on one single tiny little turtle that was just flopping his way to the water. The birds were diving down all around and picking off the younglings one by one, but this little guy insisted that he was going to make it. On the video, I can hear myself making comments about how the turtle paused for a moment as he looked around, and I wondered if this would be it. Lo and behold, he hit the water and began swimming like a real champ. The first part of his journey had been accomplished. At the same time, my camera became utterly soaked in water to the point that it was no longer functional.

One of the other travelers let me put my camera in his plastic bag, and we made our way back to the boat. By the time I got to my cabin, the camera was pretty much hosed, literally. It wouldn't power on, and I knew there wasn't much I could do about it. Thankfully, I had brought my GoPro and iPhone to also take photos while I was there. I removed the camera card from the camera and placed it on my dresser. There was no way I would let anything happen to the photos and videos I had already taken. I was delighted when I got home and found everything on the card still intact.

I can honestly say that seeing those little turtles emerge is one of the greatest highlights of my travel days. The odds of being on the right beach at the right time were staggering, but it was as if the universe was trying to tell me something. My guide had told our group that in the 19 years of his being a guide on the islands, he'd only seen that happen three times previously. To be at the birth of so much life and to literally see this happen the way I'd seen it on TV was indeed an extraordinary experience. In the grand scheme of both life and death, I would experience both of them on this trip. For now, it was time to head back to the boat and get a good night's sleep.

My third day on the islands was a bit of a mixed bag. It

started out fine when we went to Espanola. The guide nicknamed the start of our walking tour as iguana beach. There were dozens of these red and dark-colored iguanas spread out all over the rocks by the shore. Despite my camera still being out of commission, I used my iPhone to snap some pictures. When the battery finally died, I dug out the GoPro. Shortly after leaving the beach, the rain hit again. Now the shower itself wasn't cold or even that much of a problem for me. I'd traveled all that distance to see as much as I could, so I wasn't about to let the rain bother me. However, there were a few very disgruntled people on the tour that kept complaining about the rain. I remember keeping quiet about it but wanting them to shut up and just enjoy what we were getting to see.

A big part of that island was getting to see the Albatross. These birds aren't much to look at, but they are really huge. In fact, they are one of the larger flying birds in the world. My GoPro was waterproof, so I got some excellent shots of a beautiful flock of the birds sitting on the top portion of the island. We also got to see some pretty cool cliffs, waves, and an impressive geyser that was shooting pretty high due to the massive waves that day.

Unfortunately, due to the excessive complaining from some of the visitors, our guide took us back to the shore. We literally stood there, waiting for a boat to come and get us. It must have been a good 30-45 minutes of standing in the rain listening to people complain and bellyache about how they wanted back on the boat to have a drink. I found myself really annoyed by the fact that a little bit of warm rain had caused so many to start complaining. I would have been content to explore more on my own, but because of the whining, we all had to go back.

The rain did eventually ease off and allowed us to head over to what our guide referred to as "sea lion city" later in the day. The boat took us to a beach where it was literally covered in sea lions. We'd seen them in the water and on the shores of some of the smaller islands. There were islands there that people are not allowed to go to because it would represent a contamination of the wildlife that lives there. Only scientists and specific research teams were allowed to go there under certain circumstances. This particular beach was accessible to people, so off we went. Tons of these sea lions were just lying in the sun, getting some rays while everyone else stood around and took pictures with them. They'd bark at you if you got too close, and we were told not to touch them, but I probably could have put my head on one of them and used it as a pillow for an afternoon siesta.

I had charged my phone, so I sat on the beach and made a video for my wife. I told her that I missed her, and I knew that she, of all people, would have loved to have seen where I was. When I finally did get back home, I showed her the video and told her we would both return to Galapagos someday, where she could see the same things I did.

Amongst the entire island hopping, I also had the opportunity to do quite a bit of snorkeling in the water. The most memorable spot was near a rock formation nicknamed the "Sleeping Lion." It was two large rock formations with a small passageway that went between them. This area was well known for the amount of sea life that frequented the waters there. During my snorkeling excursions, I had struggled immensely to get a sense of how to properly breathe through the apparatus. So I spent most of the time holding my breath while I looked down into the water. My excursion to the Red Sea a year later would finally teach me how to properly snorkel, but for now, it was 15-30 seconds down in the water at a time.

Our guide knew the waters well, and within the time we spent there, I spotted many sharks, fish, eels, and countless others. The sharks themselves were quite large, and in fact, one hammerhead swam just meters below where I was floating. We had been told to stay clear of the rocks because if you cut yourself on the coral, the sharks would smell the blood and come for you. Although I did not experience it as I should have, being able to swim around and see the sharks and other sea life was pretty awesome.

After leaving the rocks, it was time to pack up and get ready to go. We were dropped off in San Cristobal, which was our final destination before heading back to the airport and on our way home. The small town was relatively quiet but had its share of shacks and shops to peddle various wares. I picked up a hand-carved (so they told me) tortoise and stuffed it into my bag. It would come home with me and get added to my travel shelf with the rest of the notable trinkets I've acquired during my excursions. I wandered around the coastline, watching some sea lions park themselves under cars, boats, and the docks. After about an hour exploring the area, it was time to start the trip home.

Although the time out on the water had been short, it had been well worth it. I had booked an extra day in Ecuador on purpose as I was hoping to take a day tour up to the actual equator itself to say I was there. However, those plans got cut short when I got back to the hotel and spoke to my wife for the first time since I had left home.

The entire time I was on the islands, I had no cell service. There were a few small spots where I got enough of a signal to send a message home and let the family know I was ok. When I got back to the Hilton in Quito, I finally had a chance to talk to my wife while sitting in the lobby of the hotel. Through a series of text messages, I got all of the latest updates, both good and bad.

Before I had left, my grandmother had gone into the hospital and was not in good shape. There was no expectation of her expiring anytime soon. Still, like all elderly, any illness that puts you in the hospital is a cause for concern. I opted to go on my trip despite her condition. She'd already been in and out of the hospital over the last few months. I didn't see this as being any different. Before I left, I told my wife that if something did happen, not to message me because if I did get cell service out in the middle of the water, it would have killed the entire trip.

It might sound as if I was being a bit selfish or insensitive to the situation, but that couldn't be farther from the truth. The reality was I'd be out in the middle of the ocean with no way to get back to the mainland to come home if something terrible did happen. It didn't make any sense to get a message about a death in the family when I can't return even if I had wanted to. I told my wife if anything happened to wait and tell me when I got home.

During my conversation with my wife, I knew something was up. I just felt it somehow, and as I typed on that keypad, I had to know. I told her she had to let me know if everything was ok. Then on my screen, written in blue text, it came up as "she died last night."

Somehow, I just knew this had happened and wanted to be told for sure. I finished my conversation with my wife and then immediately began to call Air Canada to find my way home early. I must have spent a couple of hours bouncing from person to person trying to find a way to get home on time to make the funeral. Eventually, I did make it to an agent who told me that they could get me as far as Toronto but not any further because of the way the flights were going. I then asked if perhaps I could get home via Montreal. I ended up paying for a one-way trip ticket from Toronto to Moncton via Montreal as an add-on to my regular return fare. Still, it did allow me to get into Moncton just before lunch, and an hour before the funeral began. I got to the funeral home much to the surprise of my mom.

This was not exactly the kind of ending I wanted for a fantastic trip, but like many things in life, there was a sense of balance that came out of it. Earlier I mentioned the birth of those turtles and seeing life and nature in its purest form. My grandmother passed away the next day, so surprisingly it really was a trip that was themed on the circle of life.

When I think of the Galapagos Islands now, I remember the tortoises, the sea lions, a couple of penguins in the water, and of course, the sea turtles that ran into the ocean as life began. I'm also reminded of my grandmother and the many memories that I have of her. It's a trip that serves as a reminder of how life is precious and that we really do need to embrace it while we can.

Feels Like Home

As a technical consultant, I spent close to six years working from an office in Moncton. Every now and then, I would be sent on the road to do technical consulting for law firms or deliver some kind of software training. In all of that time, I never had a chance to leave North America for work. The overseas trips or "good" trips, as we referred to them, only came in a handful of times a year. In those days, there was a specific pecking order for who got them, and for the longest time, I was at the bottom of that list. By the time I got to the top of the list, there were no more "good" trips left.

In 2012, I changed departments and became a full-time technical software trainer. As luck would have it, the first trip I took to shadow another trainer was to London, England. Within a couple of months of joining this new team, I had finally landed some international travel. London would become a somewhat familiar spot for me as I have been back there about six or seven times since that first excursion.

Being from Canada, I'm more familiar with the likes of Britain than some who may not be from a Commonwealth country. I remember watching Princess Diana get married on TV. I was taught in school about the Queen and Buckingham Palace and had a basic knowledge of where London was. I also knew that London and the British Colonies were steeped in history. As someone who is not much of a history buff, a lot of that historical significance is wholly lost on me. For my first and some subsequent visits to London, what stands out most is not really the same as it would be for many others.

Contrary to popular belief, what many people know as "London" is actually a combination of 32 different boroughs. These include the actual city of London as well as the city of Westminster. When you see Big Ben or the Houses of Parliament, and even Westminster Abby, they are all a part of Westminster and not the city of London itself. Typical visitors will hit the big spots right out of the gate, which I did on my first visit. I made my way via the tube to my hotel, dropped my stuff, and went exploring. The aforementioned Westminster Abby and then Buckingham Palace were the first two stops I made while exploring Greater London.

With a metro-population breaking eight million people, you would expect this would be an industrialized city like the rest of the world. Sure, it has its modern buildings and infrastructure. However, the one noticeable thing about wandering the streets of London is that it doesn't feel like a metropolis of any kind. The architecture and layout of the buildings is something else entirely. It's a city that feels like it's from another time. Block after block of stone or brick layered structures can be found. Tiny little side streets that those little cabbies zip themselves in and out of more modern streets with a contemporary building popping up every so often.

No matter where I wandered around in the city, from Westminster itself up to Greenwich, it all had a dated look and feel to it. Yet nothing seemed like it was going to crumble down at any moment. Intricate pieces of art molded into countless buildings appeared to be the norm here. Add to that the fact that the city itself seems to be in pristine condition and incredibly clean for such an active place.

There are subtle things I have found that are hard to get used to being from North America. Cars driving on the opposite side of the road didn't take long to get accustomed to, but looking the other way when I cross the street is still something I struggle with. Road signs, license plates, and even address markers themselves seem to have a "foreign" look to me as I walked from the Thames River to Buckingham Palace. Getting accustomed to their currency was another learning curve as well. England has similar money to Canada, but some of the denominations of the coin are different, so getting used to a "2 pence" and "50¢" coin took a bit of practice. Then, of course, there are the language differences you don't think of because they speak English. The subtle differences between their dialect and my Canadian English were sometimes confusing. Flat instead of an apartment; Loo instead of the washroom, and for me, the hardest one to remember was Hire instead of Rent; that one seemed to never make sense to me.

The other aspect of traveling to a European country was to see how folks overseas treated me. On the surface, most individuals would hear me speak and immediately assume I was from the United States. Although they were still friendly, for me, it always felt like they were holding back to some extent. I would then politely inform them that I was actually from Canada, and their attitude would shift. People would show a visible sigh of relief to know you weren't from the USA, even to the point of apologizing to you as if somehow calling you an American was insulting. After hearing about this kind of thing from others and questioning whether it was actually real, I was still quite surprised to see this behavior in action.

I don't know if it was because I was Canadian, or that I just felt comfortable but within a couple of days of being in London, I found myself acclimating quite well. I rode the tube like a pro (thanks in part to a great app I found to navigate my way around) and seemed to fit in with the locals quite easily. I did some geocaching in the city, which brought me to some wicked old locations, including a very tiny little pub that had been around for something like 300+ years.

Now, with so many visits to London under my belt, the most significant attractions were behind me. My subsequent visits were less than stellar despite the availability of so many things to see and do.

London is a city of history, and I'm not really a history guy. For people who love to see a city because of its historical significance, London would have to be near the top of their bucket lists of places to visit. For those such as myself, with no historical background, much of that significance is lost. Repeated visits to London now turn into an exercise of exploring new neighborhoods for the sake of seeing something new. The stories behind the buildings are lost on me, but I can still at least appreciate what I can see on the outside. Some things stick out in my mind as being more memorable than some.

On one occasion, I hopped on the tube and picked a random station to ride to and then turn around and return. I saw a great view of the sunset and the river over towards Canary Wharf. I also enjoyed attending a Comicon, where I met the cast of the television programs Haven and Warehouse 13. As a massive fan of both shows, getting to meet the actors that make the show possible was a pretty incredible experience. That same weekend I also took a bus tour to see Stonehenge, which is a fantastic monument to visit. Still, it literally is in the middle of nowhere. The trip I took brought us to Stonehenge for less than an hour as there wasn't much else to do or see there. It turns out that for the most part, you are not permitted to touch the stones unless it is a particular kind of tour for which I was not a part of. Our tour did take a trip to Bath, England, after our Stonehenge visit. We were exposed to some fantastic Roman architecture in the buildings and structures within that city.

Despite London being such an attraction within the boundaries of England, there are other parts of that region that I have had the chance to explore as well. Plymouth, located southwest of London, was a city I traveled to by train from Paddington Station and spent a week there. Like London, but on a smaller scale, it too felt like a city plucked out of history. I went up to Cardiff, Wales, for a client trip and discovered how all of the signs were written in two languages, one of which I had never heard of: Welsh. Turns out, it is still a prevalent language spoken within that region of England. I also had the opportunity to travel to Liverpool, famous for being the home to The Beatles. Liverpool had pinches of London in it but felt a lot more modern in the look and feel to the buildings and streets around it. I took a ride up on the "eye" of Liverpool and got a great view of the city at night.

Of all the trips to England and the UK, my trip to Jersey was far more memorable than many others, mainly because of the unique nature of where it is. I flew into London and then changed airports from Heathrow to Gatwick and then flew from there to Jersey. Jersey is a small island that sits on the English Channel just west of Normandy, France, and is actually closer to France than it is to England. It's not part of the UK and has its own identity, currency, and government but is protected by the UK. I spent a week in St. Helier and found myself quite enamored with the city. It's a place I had never heard of, didn't even know existed, and was in an area that I would likely have never traveled to for any reason other than work. Yet I find myself even more interested in returning there someday.

During my visit, the weather was fantastic as I never wore a jacket the whole time I was there. My hotel was perched right near the beach, and a 5-minute walk had me standing on the sand. For me, what was most striking about this place was that when the tide went out, you could walk along the floor of the ocean to Elizabeth Castle. It rests there on a tiny island, just offshore. When the tide was in, there's no way to reach the castle except by boat. One night I wandered out and walked all around the castle and just soaked everything in. I saw the most amazing sunset I'd ever experienced while sitting on the edge of one of the castle walls. I really wanted to take a ferry over to France, but the timing wasn't right, and I couldn't stay longer than my trip had been planned for. If I ever get the chance to return, I'll definitely make time to take the ferry over to see part of France.

Western Europe isn't all about England though. I've also had the pleasure of visiting Ireland several times and even Scotland for a weekend. On my first visit to Ireland, I brought my mom with me, who had wanted to see the fields of green in Ireland her whole life. Another visit saw my mother-in-law accompanying me to give her a taste of the Irish as well.

My first impression of the country came via a taxi ride from the airport in Dublin to my hotel. Having never been exposed to the Irish people firsthand in their native country, I had no idea what to expect when I got there. My driver turned out to be friendly and funny, and I spent most of the time in the cab from the airport trying not to burst out laughing at the jokes, jabs, and thick accent this man was sporting. I have very little recollection of the specifics of our conversation because his accent was so thick that most of what he said was barely legible. Between my mother and I, we just kept snickering the whole way to the hotel.

As a city, Dublin was pretty tame. The buildings and architecture reminded me of what I had seen in England. Still, again you would spot the more common areas quite easily from the parts of the city that had been around awhile. I stayed at a hotel just down the street from the Samuel Beckett Bridge. I remember the name of the bridge because that was the name of the lead character in the TV show Quantum Leap, a childhood favorite. That area was tranquil and peaceful during the evenings, and during the day, there were plenty of people walking. The River Liffey was on one side of the hotel with the Grand Canal on the other.

As I often do on my work trips, I explored a great deal of Dublin on foot. I'd see the university, McConnell Street, and a few other little spots that were within walking distance of my hotel. During one stay, my mother and I took a bus tour, which allowed us to see a lot more of the city than we had seen otherwise. Of all things in Dublin people kept telling me to do, the Guinness brewery was on the top of the list. Everyone everywhere kept telling me that I had to go see the brewery. The problem is I don't drink alcohol. *I've never had a single drop of alcohol, let alone drink a pint of beer*. So, to take a tour of a famous brewery where it's all about tasting the beer seemed to be entirely against my nature. I was told that during the brewery tour, they keep feeding you beer samples on tour, and I felt like if I went, I'd be rude by not partaking in it. Instead, the bus drove through the brewery area and provided some history to the place. That was more than enough for me.

During my visit to Dublin with my mother in tow, we took a trip to see the Cliffs of Moher. Located in western Ireland and facing the North Atlantic Ocean, the view here is remarkable. The tour left pretty early in the morning and consisted of a bus ride across the grassy plains of the country. From the window of the tour bus, it became crystal clear why Ireland is known for its green. Fields and fields of green grass and pastures littered the landscape as snow would cover the arctic. We drove across the country through the fishing town of Kinvara and Doolin Village. We even stopped at a couple of castles and the ruins of a monastery. However, the big attraction on this round of touring was the Cliffs of Moher.

Having been on the bus for most of the day, with only a little stop here and there, finally getting to the cliffs was a huge relief. After stepping off the bus and taking only a few steps towards the cliffs, everything stalled. My mother decided that the walk up to the view was "too much for her." Without going into a long sidebar about the frustrations I experienced traveling with her, I will say that she had a tendency to doubt her own capabilities. On countless occasions, she'd tell me she "couldn't" do something, but it really wasn't about not being able to do it. It was about her not thinking she could do it.

After traveling all that distance to see the cliffs, I got pretty vocal with her and told her she was doing the cliffs, whether she liked it or not. She had her hiking poles with her and could go as slow as she needed to. We took it slow and easy, and before we knew it, we were at the top of a long path, looking out at the cliffs. She smiled and said, "I did it!" She then thanked me for pushing her to take her time and go up the hill. I smiled and told her that I knew she could do it but just needed a little nudge.

She stood there looking out at the water and the cliffs below and just smiled. I told her I wanted to go for a walk down to the other side, and she was content to just stand there and look out towards the sea. I wandered over towards a "tower" of sorts and snapped a few pictures of the cliffs and the water. I, too, stopped along the edge of the wall and just looked straight out into the abyss. The cliffs themselves were pretty spectacular, but it was the view of the contrast between the green grass and the dark cliffs against the water that really stood out. When you looked down, you could see many jagged rocks and edges that would frighten anyone who happens to go over. Then, of course, you spot the crazies who go over the fence and walk down a little bit just to get a better picture despite all the warnings telling you the contrary.

For me, of all the cliffs and rocks I spotted, it was this pointy rock with what almost looked like a house sitting on top of it that stood out the most. I took the camera out and zoomed in as close as I could get. It was by no means an actual house, but the natural carving of the rock certainly made it look that way. Shortly after that, the tour ended, and it was time to return.

When my mother-in-law accompanied me to Ireland, she did the cliffs on her own but then came with me on a different tour for us to see the Giant's Causeway. The first notable difference was that we would be traveling to Northern Ireland, which is technically another country. The guide joked about us needing passports to go there, which concerned me because I didn't have mine with me, and my mother-in-law told me she had no ID with her at all. As it turned out, at least at that time, no ID is required, and there's no passport control. Northern Ireland is part of the United Kingdom, whereas the rest of Ireland is its own country. Once we hit the northern part of the country, the currency changed to pounds, and mileage switched from kilometers to miles. It was exciting hearing the long story from our guide about how the country was split in half due to religious differences and a handful of other noteworthy events.

The first notable stop on that tour was a place called Dark Hedges. If you Google Dark Hedges of Ballymoney, you'll see plenty of photos of a long street covered with Beech trees. It's a really long road with these massive trees on either side that curl over the top of the street, creating an almost tunnel that you drive or walk through. It's a popular tourist stop and has even been featured on the TV show Game of Thrones (known as the King's Road in the show). Our visit there was a quick one, but what a sight to see. The size of the trees alone was staggering, let alone how they hung over the road itself. I snapped a pile of photos and even managed to find a geocache while visiting the area.

The next stop was a place called the Carrick-a-Rede Rope Bridge. It's a famous rope bridge used to connect the mainland to a tiny little island called Carrickarede. 66' long and just less than 100' off the ground, it really is just a rope bridge suspended between two landmasses.

The walk from where the bus dropped us off to the actual bridge was about 20 minutes or so. Much like the cliffs, it had a stunning view of the water. There were no significant drop-offs here like in Moher but plenty of hills and countryside to see on one end with the water on the other.

Now, crossing the bridge itself wasn't that big a deal for me as I'm not afraid of heights. My mother-in-law was a different story. She held on tightly to the rope as we walked, and I kept my camera on video mode as I shot my entire cross of the bridge. Despite it being called a "rope bridge," it's pretty safe and secure. There was no way we were going down into the rocks below. Undoubtedly many people were too scared to traverse it. One woman had made the walk from the parking area, went down the stairs to the bridge but couldn't cross it. She was terrified.

The island, on the other side, is tiny—just enough for you to take a look at the ocean and enjoy the scenery. I went to the far end and got another tourist to take my photo in exchange for one of them with their own camera. My mother-in-law got in on it too, and we stood there looking out at the water in utter amazement.

Standing there, I found myself smiling. It wasn't the sight of the sea or the green of the island that brightened my day. I took a moment and looked at my mother-in-law as she was standing around, taking photos, and just becoming amazed by what she was seeing. She never stopped being amazed at everything we saw, no matter how small or immaterial. I took a moment to just soak in how fortunate enough I was to be here sharing it with someone else from my family. I had done the same thing the year before with my own mom, and here I was doing it again with my mother-in-law. I travel all over the world, and rarely do I get to share it with someone, so I was glad I had a chance to give this to her.

I smiled, collected her, and we headed back to the bus. The next major stop we made was the destination for this tour: the Giant's Causeway.

The legend of the causeway says that a giant named Fionn mac Cumhail was challenged to a fight by a Scottish giant by the name of Benandonner. He built the causeway across the North Channel so the two could meet. Instead of fighting, Fionn decides to hide when he sees the size of his opponent. Fionn's wife disguises him as a baby. When Benandonner sees the "baby," he becomes scared, thinking that if the baby is that big, imagine how big Fionn must be. Benandonner flees back to Scotland, destroying the causeway as he returns.

This is not a place I would have thought to go to. But since it came so highly recommended, I figured it was worth checking out. The long walk from the visitor's center down to the main beach area didn't give much of a preview of what was to come. As we inched closer to the beach area, the only thing that could be used to describe what you encounter there is "WTF?!?!"

Just a year prior, Tamara and I had seen the rocky beaches in Hawaii created by volcanic activity. Black sand beaches and countless "rocks" formed by the magma when it hardened. This area, too, was created by volcanic activity. Still, it certainly didn't look anything like what we had seen in Hawaii.

Instead, what you see is many pillars and rock formations that have a very clearly defined hexagon shape to them. Parts of me flashed back to chemistry class in high school, where they'd draw molecules on the board. You'd see H_2SO_4 drawn like little triangles or shapes with lines connecting each part of the chemical. These pillars of geometric shapes encompassed the entire area, and no matter where you looked, there they were. Even in some taller hills, you'd see cut-outs from the mountain with the same shapes formed inside.

I walked around the rock formations and kept looking down at all of these hexagons and just felt utterly bewildered by the patterns. I had more flashbacks to watching the movie Tron and the guys jumping from platform to platform when they played the "disc" game. It was as if the gods had taken a massive hexagon-shaped cookie cutter and went to town on the rocky terrain. My mother-in-law and I both just kept looking and looking, and no matter where your head turned, it was geometry class all over again.

Of all places I have been to in the world, I'd rate this the highest on the "WTF" scale. I would never have thought of traveling to a place like this, but here I was, standing in the middle of the strangest volcanic remnant ever. It's one of the few places I have been to that are the hardest to describe because it is so unique and wholly unordinary.

A quick stop at the gift shop to pick up a miniature version of the causeway itself, and we were on our way back to Dublin. The tour made a quick little stop in Belfast where we had some food, and I found a geocache. My mother-in-law got her photo taken with our bus driver, and before we knew it, we were back in Dublin, and it was time to return home.

To best summarize my experiences and thoughts of England, Ireland, and that portion of Europe, the only thing that keeps coming to mind is how that part of the world just *feels* different. In some ways, it reminds me of what my hometown is like. In many parts of Canada and the USA, it feels like we live in a fast-moving river. When you jump in, you get swept away quickly unless you know how to swim with the current. In my home province of New Brunswick, we're so laid back and friendly that we just take our time and enjoy ourselves. The parts of Europe that I have had a chance to visit thus far have felt very much the same. There are certainly plenty of places with lots of history and a pile of people. Still, for each area I have been to thus far, the sense of "rush" that we seem to experience on this side of the pond isn't present at all.

Mugged by Seagulls

Australia was a place I had wanted to visit almost as much as seeing the pyramids of Egypt. I think the appeal of going there was because it was so far away from home that I just assumed it would have to be different than where I lived. In August of 2012, I finally got the chance to see what it was all about.

At work, a blip appeared on the radar about a possible trip to Australia. The services manager was trying to determine if it made more sense to send one of his guys or send me the trainer. I said and did basically anything I could to convince him that it made more sense to send me, and sure enough, that's how it unfolded.

When I realized this trip would happen, I took a little bit of time to really consider what it was I wanted to do. I went under the assumption that I may never get back there, so I had to make the best of my time while I was there. At the same time, I also had to consider the cost of things. The Australian dollar was high compared to my own dollar at the time, so doing anything would be a bit on the pricey side.

There were really two "big" things I wanted to see that were not part of anywhere I would be for work. I knew I wanted to go scuba diving in the Great Barrier Reef, and I wanted to see the Australia Zoo made famous by the late Steve Irwin. Both of the excursions would require me to put out a chunk of coin out of pocket. I struggled a lot thinking about it and wasn't sure really what to do. Eventually, I realized that if I didn't just go for it, I would regret it. So, with a new limit on my credit card, I paid for all my excursions and never looked back.

In fact, it was that act that made me realize that moving forward, it was better to just do it than to hesitate and not do it and regret it later. I remind myself of this every time I consider the financials around travel experiences. No one wants to take on more credit card debt, but sometimes the debt is worth it. I got my Australia trip paid off in 6 months, and it was worth every penny.

For this trip, work was sending me to Brisbane for a week, and then to Sydney for an additional week. I left Moncton on a Wednesday morning, and the flight routing had me going to Toronto, then to LA, then to Sydney, then to Brisbane. Upon advice from a colleague, I took a sleeping pill on the LA-Sydney leg, and it really helped with the jetlag. When I got to Australia, I had a holdup with my luggage because I had been told it would go all the way through to Brisbane, but that wasn't the case. I was supposed to pick it up at the carousel and then drop it again. I must have spent about an hour at the airport waiting to get my bag. Eventually, I did, and I made it to Brisbane around lunchtime or so on Friday.

The class wasn't until Tuesday, but I wasn't staying in Brisbane for the weekend. I had already booked a personal flight to Cairns (pronounced Cans) for Saturday morning. The idea was for me to drop off most of my luggage, crash for the night, then get back on a plane and go to Cairns the next day, do the reef dive on Sunday, then come back to Brisbane on Monday. That first night in Brisbane was pretty tame. I spent almost the entire time in bed just sleeping and relaxing, trying to acclimate to the time zone. There was a 13hr time difference between Moncton and Brisbane. By the time I got up Saturday, I was good to go.

Cairns is a couple of hours by air, and I quickly made my way from the airport to the Heritage Cairns hotel. Settled in for the night and anxiously awaited the morning where I would head out to the Great Barrier Reef.

Early Sunday morning, I got up and headed out on my tour of the reef around 7:15am. I got picked up and brought to the dock where many other tourists also got on board. This was really the first "boat" tour I had ever taken anywhere. I'd been on my grandfather's fishing boat many times as a kid, but it wasn't quite the same thing as this.

The tour company, Reef Trip, gave all of us the lowdown on what to expect and how things would go. We mostly had a couple of different spots we would go diving and snorkeling. Everyone had to fill out a medical/registration form, which is where things got a little uneasy for me.

I had done a lot of reading about scuba diving and asthma. As someone who has asthma, there seemed to be a mixed opinion on whether it is safe for someone with asthma to go scuba diving. I had been very adamant in ensuring my asthma was under control and hadn't had any attacks in months. The medical advisors on the boat were insistent that the possibility existed that some people with lung issues can die as a result of using the scuba equipment when an asthma attack occurs.

I contemplated lying on my form about having asthma but got kind of spooked by what they said, so I went the honest route. As a result, I never got a chance to scuba. I have since learned that people with asthma can go scuba diving, but they need to have a letter from a specialized doctor that indicates you are safe to dive. It really depends on your lung capacity and how your asthma is triggered. I think I'd be ok now, but who's to say for sure.

I did get to go snorkeling. However, this was my first time ever experiencing snorkeling. I ended up struggling to breathe correctly through the tube. Not because of any physical issues, but simply because I kept panicking every time I tried to breathe. So instead of doing real snorkeling, I held my breath each time I put my face in the water. It wasn't great for being able to see for long periods, but it was still pretty cool, and I did get to see plenty.

I do remember that I wore a wetsuit for my excursions, and I remember clearly how warm the water felt when I jumped in. I had never felt the water that warm before in my life. I don't know if it was the actual water temperature itself. Or just because I wore a wetsuit, but I will say that the wetsuit definitely helped me from getting cold after I got out of the water.

I did opt for an underwater digital camera as I didn't own a GoPro at the time. So I did get some great photos from beneath the surface of the water. Not as lovely as some of the ones I spotted from those who got to go scuba diving, but still pretty nice. Looking back at it now, I wish I had known how to properly snorkel as I would have enjoyed the time a lot more than I did. I remember feeling a bit underwhelmed by the experience but mainly because I didn't get to scuba. The snorkeling wasn't quite what I wanted it to be but still an incredible experience. The next time I go, I'll be better prepared to snorkel and will be able to see a lot more. At the end of the day, I got to experience the Great Barrier Reef, which was something I had never expected to be able to do.

During the trip back to shore, the boat was flying through the water at quite a high speed. It was going so fast that below deck, there was a lot of crashing of water and waves hitting the windows. It was loud and very cool to see. I also have a vivid memory of someone who was on the upper level that got seasick because they puked over the side of the deck. Those of us inside saw chunks cover one of the windows. As gross as it was, it gave us below deck quite a laugh.

After a full day at sea, I fell asleep quite early at the hotel, and the time change had me up before dawn. I went for a really early morning walk along the beach and snapped many photos of the water, the sand, and the sky. Later in the day, I did a bit of exploring in the local area. I wandered around to just see what I could, then headed back to the hotel and eventually back to the airport to head over to Brisbane.

I spent a week in Brisbane, and I think there's a part of me that wants to say I enjoyed it more than Sydney. In retrospect, I actually did a lot more in Sydney than I did anywhere else in Australia. Still, the skyline of Brisbane by the water and some of the buildings at night really gave it a beautiful look.

I took some time while I was there to go for a walk and enjoy the area. I stayed at a nice hotel called the Sebel Suites, which was downtown but very close to the botanic gardens. From the hotel, I took a nice walk south to the gardens and enjoyed a lovely view of the docks. From there, you could spot the river and some of the skyline as well. As I walked through the wooded area, there were many trees where people had carved initials into them. I smiled, grabbed a small rock, and cut my own MK + TK initials into a tree. Tamara may not have been with me, but she left her mark with me in that park. Maybe someday we'll both return and see if the initials are still there.

I crossed the Goodwill Bridge, a lovely little walking bridge between the gardens and the South Brisbane War Memorial Park. I enjoyed the walk along the river, taking in some of the exciting pieces of sculpture art that had been left near there. Someone had used an old cement pillar and placed a metal sculpture on it that looked like a stork. I sat on the edge of the river, looked over at the city, and just enjoyed the fact of where I was. Like many of the other places I would visit later, I just soaked in the experience of being so far away from home.

The rest of the week was mainly worked related. I took time each night to go out for a walk and wander around the streets to see what I could find. There was an excellent area for shopping, some government offices, and a considerable share of high rise buildings, along with a non-descript strip club just around the corner. I smiled when I saw the entrance but opted to keep on walking. I took a walk towards Waterfront Place during the evening. Some of my best photographs of downtown were snapped there. There's a real nice walkway that sits behind many taller office structures and runs along the river. You could even take a water taxi across the river or keep on walking up towards Story Bridge and cross there as well.

Beyond wandering downtown, I didn't get much further, and before I knew it, Saturday came. It was time to go for a completely different type of adventure: driving on the opposite side of the road.

I stayed in Brisbane over the weekend because I knew that I wanted to go to the Australia Zoo. This is a zoo made famous by the aforementioned late Steve Irwin, aka the Crocodile Hunter. In my mid-20s, I was a massive fan of him, so when I knew I'd be in Australia, I had hoped I could get a chance to visit the zoo itself. I booked a car rental with a pickup spot not far from my hotel and snagged it on Saturday morning. Keys in hand, the real fun was about learning to drive all over again.

Australia drives on the left, which means the driver's side is on the right. This is, of course, entirely backward to how we operate in Canada, and I had never driven that way before. It took me a moment once I got in the car to orient myself correctly. Before I left home, I had read an article about learning to drive on that side, and one thing stuck out more than anything else. It suggested you do your best to have someone in front of you to follow until you get the hang of it. Well, I got out of the garage on my own just fine and then waited until a car passed, and I started to follow it.

Within a couple of minutes, the whole "backward" thing felt kind of familiar. In fact, the entire driving experience was pretty painless. I spent most of my time just fighting my instincts to try and train my head to drive in their correct lane. What I struggled with the most was getting the turn signals mixed up with the wipers because they were on opposite sides of the steering column. I can't tell you how many times I turned the wipers on by accident when I was trying to turn.

I made my way up north to the zoo pretty quickly, and before I knew it, I was there.

When I think about visiting that zoo, there are only a handful of things that really stood out. Road signs along the way showed photos of Steve Irwin telling you that you were getting closer. The zoo itself was very typical. Lots of animals and attractions filled the place. There was a massive display in the middle of the zoo dedicated to Steve Irwin. It was filled with lots of photographs and memorabilia of the man and his legacy he left his family and the world.

For the wildlife, sure there were a ton of animals that I took photos of that I couldn't tell you today what they were. They did have a large kangaroo section where they wandered around freely, and you could go in there and interact with them. I fed a bunch and got some pictures with them. They were friendly enough that you could pet them, but you still had to be careful.

The koala exhibit was pretty impressive. Those are some of the cutest animals you can possibly imagine, and I really did want to pick one up and take it home. I learned that even though people call them koala bears, they aren't bears at all and sleep almost 20hrs a day.

There was an entertaining crocodile show, but nothing that really stood out for me as being spectacular. I did get a picture taken with a giant snake around me, which was also kind of cool.

At the end of that excursion, I found myself quite happy with what I had seen and was glad to have made the trek. Now it was time to head back and make my way to Sydney.

A quick little flight on Monday morning had me arriving in Sydney just after 8am. I made my way to the hotel, dropped my bags off, and wandered. The first target for me was to find the famous Sydney Opera House. Of all the buildings in Australia, the opera house is probably the one building that stands out beyond the rest as being a symbol of Australia and Sydney in particular. I got a few photos of the opera house itself, along with one or two of me with it in the background. Oddly enough, I also saw camels hanging out in the park near there. I found it funny that I'd travel as far as Sydney to find camels there. It seemed utterly opposite to what I would have expected.

The real mission of wandering, aside from wanting to see what was there, was to find out where the bridge climb was. A colleague of mine had told me that you can actually pay a fee and walk on the steel girders of the Sydney Harbour Bridge. I took the same approach to this as I did for the reef tour. I knew it would be expensive, but I also knew that I may never get the chance to do it again. I booked a climb to happen just in time to catch the sunset while at the top. A lot of people online had recommended that time, so I went for it.

Now what you need to know about the climb is that they put you in a jumpsuit, attach a special harness which you clip to as you climb. You are not permitted to bring anything with you, including cameras. At the time, they took photos of you as you ascend and descend, and you receive one of those photos (of your choice) as part of the standard package. You can pay for more photos, or you can pay for a USB stick and get them all. Again, knowing I would not be back, I said the hell with it and paid the $120 Australian Dollars for the USB stick. It was a ridiculous amount of money for a few photos, but "when in Rome" stuck out in my mind. The pictures I did get from their package were quite beautiful. I'll also add that I think they offer photo downloads now.

For the climb itself, you start off in a room under the bridge, and then precisely as advertised, you slowly ascend up one side towards the arch. A few stops along the way to enjoy the view and get some photos taken, eventually, you get to the crest of the bridge, and you really do enjoy the view from there. I got my best pictures of myself in Sydney from the top of that bridge. Really well done and, in my opinion, absolutely worth every penny I spent. You then make your way down the other side of the bridge, and before you know it, it's all done.

For the rest of the week, I worked my days and explored downtown at night. I didn't go too far, but I always wandered around as far as I could each evening as long as I felt up to it. Having to teach programming all day took a lot out of me, so I didn't get as far as perhaps I would have liked, but I made do. I spent a lot of time taking photos near the water and around the opera house. I even took a little boat tour to see the harbor from one side of the bridge all the way under it and far past the opera house closer to Shark Island. I got some great photos and views of the bridge and opera house from the boat tour. It was certainly worth spending a little money on it.

Of course, I also experienced my "mugging," as depicted in the first chapter of this book. None of the evenings of wandering around downtown Sydney stood out for me except for that one simply because the nature of it was so funny.

On my last day of "work," a bunch of us went out for drinks, and I had a conversation with one of the students I had been working with. She was a really smart, quite beautiful looking young woman whom I still reference in my programming classes from time to time. In talking to her, it was quite clear that the folks from "down under" were just like everyone else I had met in many places across the globe. We talked about work, our lives, our families, and all of the things that really matter. I actually remember telling her about the fact that I usually hated going to "social" outings with colleagues because, for the most part, I'm pretty socially awkward. All the folks from that office made it pretty easy to unwind and just be yourself. I said my goodbyes, walked out, headed back to my hotel, and knew I had one last day in Sydney before making the long haul home.

Saturday was a "tour" day. I had booked a city tour to see as much of Sydney as I could. I've done these tours for other cities, and I knew that I wasn't going to see as much as I wanted to if I tried to do it on my own. So, I got on a bus and did the very typical "tourist" thing.

There were plenty of stops on tour, but not a lot of which stand out in mind as being "amazing" or life-shattering. Like most city tours, they took us all to places that most visitors want to see. I managed to get to both Bondi and Manly beaches, both of which were amazing to see. There was a park not far from the opera house that we made a stop at. On the easternmost tip of the park was "Mrs. Macquarie's Chair." This was a sandstone sculpture where the wife of a famous governor of New-South Wales would sit and watch the harbor for ships from Great Britain. The park itself wasn't all that notable, but the carved "chair" in the rock was pretty cool.

The guide took us to a spot on the other side of the river to see the bridge from the other side. We also ended up in a place where we were elevated relatively high and could see the water and cliffs from our position. There was a park there where we could wander around and take photos. I got some of the sweetest cliff photos with water crashing against the rock.

The only other notable spot that I visited that day was the Arabanoo lookout in Dobroyd Head. It was a beautiful view of the water and landscape, but the history of Arabanoo was what struck me. The British wanted to study the indigenous population. He was the first of his kind to be captured and analyzed by the British in 1788. The story goes that he had helped others with smallpox but caught the disease himself and then later died from it. I remember wondering what it would have been like for the original British settlers to encounter individuals such as him and what they thought of them.

The day ended with me returning to my hotel, packing up, and starting the trip home. I had a 13.5hr flight from Sydney to San Francisco, on which I spent most of it asleep. I struck up a conversation with the young woman sitting beside me who was moving from Sydney to San Francisco to become a nanny. I'm not typically one to chat with folks on the plane, but she asked me about how I was able to sleep on the flight, and the conversation went from there.

The plane landed, and I pondered what to do. I had an 8.5hr layover in the city, so I stored my bag and wandered. I took a trolley car downtown and eventually ended up at Fisherman's wharf. I snapped some photos, got a good laugh at the Bush Man (look him up on Google), then headed back to the airport for my next flight. I took a redeye from San Francisco to Newark and had a 13hr layover there. I hadn't slept a lot but didn't want to sit in the airport for that long, so I stored my bag again and went into NYC. I had never walked the Brooklyn Bridge, so I thought this was a perfect time to do it. I got across the bridge and had intended to take a subway to midtown but discovered that fatigue was finally catching up with me. I went back to the airport and vegged/slept in the lounge until my flight to Moncton left. I got home just after 11pm and where I was greeted by my wife and son. I was happy to finally be back in my own bed.

I have not had the pleasure of returning to Australia since that first trip, but I plan to travel there with my wife when we turn 50. What I do know now is that my initial expectation of Australia was a complete miss from reality.

For some reason, I had this idea since I was a kid because Australia was so far away from home, it had to be different than here. You think of these places that are so far away and begin to assume that the people and the life they have there must be different. This was another example of how everyone across the globe has a common thread. The lifestyle down there was not much different than it was back in my hometown. Cars, technology, food, clothing, and most of what I was used to was basically the same. The money looked different, and the people talked with an accent. But they were really no different than I. I've since traveled to other parts of the world and have learned that it didn't seem to matter where I went; people were the same everywhere.

Escapism at Its Finest

Las Vegas is well known for many things. Still, for those who have not had the opportunity to actually visit, you need to know that there is a reason it's called Sin City.

Las Vegas is filled with gambling, smoking, drinking, stripping, partying, sex, and all things considered to be "illicit" in one form or another. It's a city where people can drink alcohol out in the open, so seeing someone with a giant margarita wandering the streets is normal. You can smoke inside any building at any time. Prostitution is illegal in Clark County (where Las Vegas resides), but that doesn't stop the cars advertising "girls to you" up and down the strip. Legal brothels like Sheri's Ranch are just a quick drive away. For the right price, you can get your rocks off at an adult strip club. You can go fire guns of any kind in the many gun ranges throughout the city. How about hopping in a race car and drive around a track at 200mph? Get in a fighter jet and have a simulated air combat battle. Or if you'd rather just see the pretty girls and take some photos, go for a walk along the strip. People go to the Caribbean to see the beaches and lay back in the sun doing as little as possible. Vacations in faraway lands allow you to experience history and culture beyond your hometown. Most that opt to spend time in Las Vegas are there to escape the real world and live in a playground where nothing seems to be off-limits.

In the summer of 1997, I stopped in Las Vegas overnight on my way to Los Angeles. I did a couple of drives up and down the "strip," accompanied by a quick five-minute game on the slots in the old Stardust hotel, which has long since been demolished, and that was enough for me. Since then, I've been back to Vegas several times, and they all have shared a common theme: escapism.

In 2009, my wife and I took a trip to Vegas for a few days just to see the sights. Our daughter had been born in April of that year, and it had been a rough few months. I love her dearly, and she's a sweetheart now, but she was not a happy baby in the early days. My wife and I both desperately needed a break, so Las Vegas seemed like a perfect place to go and forget the world behind us.

I booked a room at the Bellagio, which turned out to be a pretty lovely suite. I opted to spend a little bit more money than I really should have but given how rough the last few months had been, I just really needed to splurge a bit on us. The suite was more significant than any room I had stayed in at the time. Something I found in the bathroom actually served as the inspiration for a Christmas gift I bought my wife a few years later.

I had bought tickets to see the "O" show, so on our way to it, we explored a little bit further around the hotel and eventually came to the theater. We checked out part of the "gallery" area, which was really just a bunch of art pieces tied to the show itself. Before we knew it, the doors opened, and it was time to get seated.

The show itself is fantastic. I cannot fathom the training those performers have to go through to make that show happen, but it was mind-boggling. I'm not one for musicals or any of that "artsy" type of performance shows, but this was an absolutely fantastic show to see. It's really an excellent combination of the use of water and acrobatics you could ever imagine. Since then, I have seen some other shows in Vegas, and I still think that "O" is the best. It's also a show that starts off with some audience participation, which adds to the allure. We walked away from it with an inflatable life preserver from the act, making it that much more memorable.

Vegas is well known for its shows, but buyers beware. There are plenty of places that will offer up discounted or even free tickets to a show, but many times these shows are the smaller ones which are not all that great. I've seen a few performed at one of the theatres at the Miracle Mile, and you can definitely tell the difference in caliber compared to the larger scale shows. It's okay if you want to see what it's about, but try and remember that you get what you pay for.

A big part of visiting Vegas is all about going in and out of the hotels. The strip itself is littered with big, flashy hotels, and every one of them has something different to offer. There's an Atlantis show at Caesar's Palace and the famous fountains of the Bellagio. The New York New York Hotel features a roller-coaster, and even the Secret Pizza restaurant can be found at Aria. They all offer something unique for visitors to see. Every time you come back, there's always something new and different about each of these places that draws you in.

Unbeknownst to many, Vegas actually started out downtown, and there is still a lot to see down there, including what is one of the other more memorable attractions in the city. Freemont Street is an open walking area downtown that is entirely covered by this light show. To call it a light show is actually insulting. It's so much more than just a bunch of lights flickering. It's an entire canopy of lights and displays that run for several city blocks. Every hour during the evening, a "show" is performed with music blasting and the light show going along with it. Bands play on stages outside, with buskers doing spray paint art, and more men and women dressed in as little as they can just to get you to tip them for a photo. The strip may be where a lot of the flash is, but Freemont feels more like where the party really begins. No visit to Las Vegas is complete without enjoying a little over-indulgent partying in downtown Sin City.

Freemont Street is also home to Slotzilla, a zip line that runs from one end of the street to the other. Passengers go up several flights of stairs where they are attached to a harness and laid down on their stomachs. It propels you forward and across a zip line from one end of the party all the way to the other. There are actually two different versions of the zip line. One of them starts halfway, and you just hang on while the other one is a horizontal zip line where you fly like Superman. Having done the latter, I can tell you that it's a great experience even if you only ever do it once.

During another visit to Vegas, I was slated to spend a week there for work. Our yearly conference is always an experience unto itself. Then throw a party city like Vegas into the mix, and it was sure to make for an exciting week. When booking some travel for another work trip, I was asked if I wanted to do a short survey over the phone for one of the Hilton resorts I had stayed at. Within a few minutes, I got roped into a deal to spend three nights at the Elara in Vegas in exchange to go to one of those timeshare meetings. The price was right, and I knew I'd be there within a particular window, so I left for Vegas a few days early with my wife in tow.

During our excursion around the city, we stopped at the Stratosphere Tower. This is the Vegas version of the CN Tower or Seattle Space Needle. It's a giant tower with an observation deck on top. We had secured a free visit to the upper floor, and as we wandered around, I noticed that they now had the option to jump from the deck to the ground below. For years they had touted their "rides" at the top, which were basically these psyche-out rides that either shot and pulled you back or hung you over the edge. We'd seen them the last time we were there. In addition to the rides, they added a new attraction. They actually had a rig that allowed you to jump right off the top of the tower while attached to a harness. It's mostly a controlled freefall, but you still go over the edge.

We stood by the window and watched person after person jump, and every time they went, my wife's heart skipped a beat from fear, while mine skipped a beat with excitement. I never even thought twice about it before deciding to go and get my ticket to jump.

It was about $100 for the jump and another $25 for the camera after the discounts we got, but the price was worth it. They put you in a jumpsuit and strap the camera to your arm. You then take the elevator up to the top and are escorted out to the jumping area. They weigh you to calibrate the rope, and then when given the cue, they take your photo and walk you out to the jump platform. There are two ropes attached to you: the main harness and a backup. As you go outside, they get you to hold onto the outside rail, and they hook you up to the central harness and point you right out at the Vegas strip. The guy there asked me to use my camera to show where I was. I took my right arm, which the camera was attached to, and pointed it out towards the Vegas Strip. From the spot I stood at, the strip was clearly visible directly in front of me as I moved the camera around to give people a sense of how far up I was. I stood on the platform, and he held the back of my tether with me leaning forward just a bit. After counting down, he let go, gave me a small push, and off I went.

Honestly, every time I watch the video, I try and remember what it was like. I remember I wasn't scared at all; I was really excited. The freefall was pretty tame, and the entire jump was over in a minute with a nice graceful landing on the bottom. My wife, however, couldn't hold the camera up from the ground to shoot the video of me, so she had her head turned the whole time while someone else filmed the video. I laughed when she told me about it later. Then we found out that they'd allow you to do a second jump for half price if you went back within 24hrs. So, that same night, I went back again and did the plunge a second time. This time though, I hatched a plan.

When I go to my yearly work conference, it's really tiring. I get up early and have breakfast with my colleagues. I work all day, giving presentations and helping customers, and then devote my entire evenings to hanging out with my co-workers. I love the team I am on, but when you spend all day, and then all evening, with the people you work with, it kind of feels like you are working the entire day. Despite being able to kick back and enjoy yourself in the evenings, conversations always end up turning towards work, so it really makes for long, tiring days. I wanted to make sure that this time around, I wasn't just sitting around waiting for everyone else to figure out what to do. I wanted to take the reins and make something cool happen.

If you get the GoPro for your jump, they film a little intro of you before you jump and ask you a few questions, including if you have any last words before you leap. For my second attempt, I issued a challenge to all of my co-workers who would be in town that week to do the same jump. I then posted it on Facebook and tagged every single person I worked with that I had on Facebook. Many people accepted the challenge, but when the time came, we had 8 people from our company, including me, go up and do the jump. When I did the drop this time, the guy at the top recognized me from my last two drops and let me actually do a little real jump off the platform edge. I didn't film that jump, but I think it was my favorite because I really did jump, and I descended on Vegas at nighttime instead of the day.

As for my colleagues, the best part of watching them go was the last guy to do the jump. He was the one who was the most scared of it, and when he jumped, he let out one of the girliest screams I've ever heard a grown man make. He was so embarrassed by the shriek he wouldn't post his video on Facebook. He was glad he did the jump but quite mortified by his yelp.

My wife had no interest in jumping. She did however have a pretty big fascination in crossing the street and shooting some guns. Vegas has a reputation for having some pretty wicked gun ranges where you can shoot anything you want. I had no interest in paying money to shoot some artillery, but for some reason, my wife really wanted to try it. We went over and got a package that allowed her to shoot three different guns. The first one was a little handgun, and the second one was a more like a shotgun. The last gun was a nice sized machinegun, which I believe was an M249. I'm not a gun guy, but the gunsmith brought this thing out, propped it up on the counter, and showed her how to use it. I stood back and shot a video of her as she pulled the trigger for the first time, and a short burst of bullets sprayed out at the target. The sound and rapid-fire caught me off guard, and I said to the gunsmith, "Holy f*ck," for which he turned around, looked at me with a grin, and then just nodded at me.

She then pulled the trigger and unloaded the last of her ammo on the target. When she backed up from the gun, she was giggling uncontrollably, shaking. She proceeded to say, "That was awesome!!!" in one of the highest-pitched voices I had ever heard her exclaim. It's one of my fondest memories of that trip to Vegas.

She was allowed to keep some of the shells from the gun, so we brought them home. I remember wondering if the airport security would screen the bag and ask questions about why we had machine gun shells in our luggage.

There was one gun that was on display in the window that did look a bit appealing to me, but the price tag was too steep. I have no idea what the actual gun was called (it may have been a Browning M3), but I just referred to it as the BFG (taken from the videogames Doom & Quake), which stood for "big f*cking gun." The thing was huge, and the belt-fed bullets looked like mini-rockets, but I wasn't prepared to fork out more than $500 to shoot off 30 rounds from this one gun. Had I scored big at the casino, though, I may have considered it.

On another day, we did take an afternoon and go for a little excursion outside of the city. There's plenty of things to do and see in town, but we opted to take a short day trip north. As a geocacher, I was well versed in a very famous "power trail" that exists about 90 minutes north of Las Vegas. In geocaching, a power trail is a trail of geocaches where a cache has been hidden every 161 meters (.1 miles) along a route. There's a famous power trail on Highway 375 (known as the ET Highway) that runs through Rachel, Nevada, with 1500 geocaches on it. For many people into geocaching, that trail is a destination of choice because you can get a lot of geocaches in a short time along a singular route.

Add to that the fact that a few roads off that main highway

lead you to the even more infamous Area 51. It's technically a detachment of Edwards Air Force Base. It has been linked to countless stories of UFO activity in the skies above it. Even if you don't know the intricate details of Area 51, you've probably heard the term mentioned once in a while through pop culture. As an avid sci-fi fan and lover of all things alien-related, Area 51 seemed like a neat spot to go see given how close it was to Las Vegas.

We took a trip up to Rachel, NV, to see what this was all about. The road itself is pretty lonely, and virtually no services on that highway, so be sure to have lots of gas before turning onto 375. I found 100 or so geocaches on the road, but with the heat as hot as it was in mid-June, I wasn't doing a lot more of them. We made a stop at a very famous "Inn" known as the Little A'Le' Inn. It's a tiny little inn/restaurant in the middle of nowhere but has been shown on countless TV shows and movies for years. We stopped in, had some food, bought a few souvenirs (including a map to Area 51), and then headed over to where the boundary of Area 51 is.

There's not much to see as far as this secret base is concerned since you can't get very close, but all the stuff you hear about the trucks on the hill, cameras watching you, and the line you can't cross are all true. We came to a spot on the dirt road where plenty of signs were visible that told us that if we were to go any further, we would be arrested. Clearly visible on the right side of the "boundary" line and up on a hill was a white truck parked looking down on us. They never came down, but word is if you cross that line, they will bolt and come to get you. I had one visit where after leaving the boundary area on my way back to the highway, two of those trucks *flew* past me. They were obviously trying to get somewhere in a hurry, but they never bothered me.

Despite not seeing anything of real interest, it was still cool to be near something that's got such a reputation behind it. I suspect all that goes on in there is building refrigerators or smoking dope all day or something else just as mundane. Still, it is fun to imagine the kinds of crazy things that could be going on in there. There's even a legend that an alien by the name of J'Rod works there. It certainly does inspire the imagination.

The surprising thing about being out there, though, was how quiet and peaceful it was. There are cactus and desert everywhere, but virtually no one around to bother you. You could just sit back and enjoy being out in the open air. There were moments just standing out there that it kind of reminded me of what it was like being in the desert of Jordan. The terrain was different, but the feeling of calmness and quiet surroundings was definitely the same. After getting one of my last geocaches during a solo visit to the area, I parked my car on a desert road, pointed it west, and watched the sun go down. It was a peaceful moment in literally the middle of nowhere, but so quiet and memorable.

In my visits to Vegas, there's always a common theme. Wander the strip, explore the hotels, go to Freemont St, explore that area, have some food, and in one form or another, find a way to indulge yourself. One often overlooked aspect of Vegas is that it offers the unique opportunity to take a vacation from yourself. This is a city where people go to be crazy and do all things over the top. You can't go to a place like that and just expect to be nothing more than yourself. It's almost as if it's a requirement to forget who you really are and just break free. Of course, had I done that, I probably would have come home to divorce and mandatory AA meetings. For me, the closest I got to stretching myself was to find a way to overcome some of my social anxiety. Vegas seemed like the right place to try it out.

Whether you're on the strip or downtown, you're bound to see people in costume looking for you to tip them for a photo. It's become quite popular in places like New York City, but in Vegas, it can be a bit more extreme. You'll see a few people in cartoon character costumes, but by far and large, it's girls in showgirl outfits, playboy bunnies, or naughty cops. The girls show off their "assets" in hopes of getting tips for photos with the passersby. For me, it's a guilty pleasure. I'm a very happily married man who would never step out on his wife. But what straight guy doesn't like to see a pretty girl dressed in something provocative and know that looking is not going to get you into trouble? Again, this is Sin City, and the provocative nature of the city is everywhere.

I've always been intimidated by beautiful women. Walking up to a gorgeous woman in a barely legal cop uniform is something that is entirely outside of my comfort zone on so many levels. Yet if the wife were with me, she'd be the one asking the cop for the photo. During one excursion to Vegas, I pretended to be the confident guy who doesn't get scared by these dazzling women, and I got a pile of photos taken. In fact, one of my favorite pictures from that trip involved two sets of showgirls. Each pair of girls used my camera to snap each other's photos with me. While one of them was fixing her outfit, the other two had my camera. Since I was distracted, they took a hilarious selfie that I didn't know about until I loaded the pictures up later that day. I got home and showed the photos to my wife, and she was all proud of me finding a way to be less shy. To some people, it might sound a bit lame, but for me, being able to step out of my comfort zone and do something like that was a big deal.

And no, the irony is not lost on me. Jumping off a building or out of an airplane is nowhere near as scary as asking a pretty girl for a photograph. I know many people where the opposite would be true. Everyone is different.

When I think of my experiences in Vegas, I think of the excessiveness of the city. I think of the pretty girls and the lavish hotels. I think of my wife shooting guns and me jumping off buildings. I think of a helicopter ride that showed the beautiful lights of the city at night. I think of the oddball encounters with other tourists who ended up being from the same little Canadian town as me. I remember my wife and I experienced a bit of the naughty side of Vegas in a now-closed down cabaret club. I recall standing on Las Vegas Blvd in front of the Bellagio, just watching all of the people around. Every one of them had a story about what brought them to Vegas. I wondered if any of theirs was the same as mine.

For all of what the city offered, I never found myself feeling unsafe, or really that unhappy. As long as I embraced what was around me, the town seemed to really open up. Las Vegas truly is a town for escapism. When you need to get away from the ins and outs of your daily life and just want to go somewhere that's got plenty to do and is soaked in excess, Sin City is the place.

Lastly, for all the time I spent in Vegas, gambling would be at the bottom of the list of things I did. Sure, I played a few rounds of blackjack and would drop a bit of coin in a slot machine, but spending my money trying to win even more was never what Vegas was about.

It's all about going over the top and just escaping the world, even if it is only for a short time.

Lost in Paradise

I knew that my 10th anniversary was coming up, so I wanted to do something a little extra special. Most of my vacation days had already been booked, so I was trying to find a time of the year that would be slow at work. Late November seemed to be the best time as it was Thanksgiving in the US, and that week is always quiet. I booked the time off for that week and started looking for a beautiful place to spend our anniversary.

My wife had said before that she'd like to go somewhere tropical and just relax. Most of the trips we had taken were always jam-packed with things to do or see, mainly because I didn't want to sit around. For our anniversary, I thought I'd try and compromise and find somewhere nice we could just relax.

Trying to find a tropical place to visit in late November is not an easy task. In fact, most of the all-inclusive locations were either closed or indicated that it wasn't a good idea to visit them during

November because of the weather. I looked and looked and looked and came up with nothing. While scouring through countless travel websites, I spotted something about Hawaii. They mentioned that it's always beautiful year-round. The bell went off in my head, and I started researching. Sure enough, it was true. There would be mild chances of rain but nothing so severe that I should be concerned. That was enough for me to pick Hawaii as our anniversary destination.

I booked a week at the Hilton Hawaiian Village Waikiki Beach Resort hotel. As a business traveler, I had accumulated a ton of Hilton points. I was able to get the entire week for no charge. Paid for the flights and a rental car, and all was set. Now we just had to actually get there.

Traveling from Moncton to Honolulu is a long trek. We flew from Moncton to Montreal, Montreal to Vancouver, and then Vancouver to Honolulu. We spent about 4-5 hours in Vancouver visiting with one of our long-time friends we hadn't seen in years. However, leaving Moncton at 5:45am and getting to Hawaii at 9:45pm (with a 6hr time change) was a really long travel day. We got off the plane, grabbed our bags and rental car, and made our way to the hotel.

The drive itself was somewhat dull, but not because of the city. It was annoying because we were exhausted and just wanted to rest. I barely paid attention to much of anything until we found ourselves at the hotel.

We got upgraded to a larger room, and thanks to my wife and her wheeling and dealing, we got the parking charge waived. Off to our room we went, unloaded our bags, and then crashed for the night. It was an exhausting trip, and we knew we had plenty of time to enjoy the week we had there.

The next morning, we made our way downstairs and started to explore the resort. There were plenty of places to eat, shop, and enjoy the sights and sounds of the area. For lunch, we tried Tropics Bar & Grill, where we ordered this sushi sampler, which came with several different types of sushi. My wife had enjoyed a lot of sushi before, but I was a bit reluctant to dive in. Since it was something the locals ate a lot of, I took a deep breath and went for it. Turns out, it was a lot better than I had imagined. We had ordered a large platter for the two of us, so at first, it was fine, but after eating a lot of it, we both found ourselves wanting to finish up and explore some more.

From there, we spent quite a bit of time exploring around the resort we were at on the first day. It was right on Waikiki beach, so we made sure to spend some time there. We didn't go too far on that first day as we just wanted to acclimate to the environment. A 6hr time difference between home and Hawaii also made it harder to get used to where we were. That first full day was really more about acclimating and resting than anything else.

On Sunday, we went for a drive around Honolulu and spotted the Pearl Harbor museum. We took a look at the grounds but opted not to go in and then took a trip to the North Shore of the island, known for its beaches and surfing. With no specific destination in mind, we drove around to get a sense of what there was to see. Unbeknownst to my wife, I was steering us towards Waimea Falls in hopes we could visit there.

As it turned out, we'd end up back in that same general area later in our visit when we'd do our LOST tour. For now, we made the occasional stop to see a beach along the side of the road. There were plenty of little spots to stop and take some photos of the big waves.

Driving along Route 83, it became pretty apparent which areas were more famous for swimming and beach time. The streets were lined with parked cars for those wanting to go for a dip in the ocean. We stopped in one spot where there was nowhere to park the car, but somehow we managed to squeeze in between a couple others who had avoided a large puddle on the ground. For us, we didn't care if we had to dodge a few wet spots here and there. After crossing the street, we wandered down to the beach, took some photos, enjoyed the sun, and came back to the car to head to our next spot.

I actually had looked up a place in the North Shore called Waimea Falls. In the TV show LOST, the waterfalls from this area had been used for several episodes, and from what I could tell, it was a pretty nice area to go visit.

It had started to sprinkle rain a bit when we arrived, so I grabbed the GoPro camera and used it for most of the photo-taking. We knew that the time of year we were visiting would bring rain at some point, but we didn't really care. Both of us were just happy to be in paradise.

After parking the car at the entrance, we paid our fare, and my wife made friends with a beautiful peacock who was wandering the grounds. She's always been fascinated by those birds. She did anything and everything she could to get in as close to the animal as possible. Even after we did the entire tour of the area and were eating, she was still going around taking photos of the bird. Chickens and roosters were wandering around as well, but the peacock really stood out.

The walk to the falls is a gentle, pleasant little stroll through the woods. Some of the leaves of the trees were almost as big as I was. The hiking path took us to a miniature village and down to a stream that went through the area. The vegetation wasn't anything like you would see back home. Green and green and greener everywhere, but it wasn't pine and spruce trees. Some of the trees themselves were massive, with giant branches that seemed to spread out for miles.

Tamara was quite taken by some of the flowers we spotted. We even managed to find a small tree that had wild bananas growing out of it. We plucked one and kept it, but as I recall, I don't think it tasted very well by the time we tried to eat it.

Eventually, we came to the end of the path where the actual waterfall was. It was indeed the same one I had seen on LOST, so for me, it was really cool to be in that spot. We had the option to jump in and go swimming at the base of the falls. Neither of us had worn or brought a swimsuit. Instead, we watched a few others take on the waterfall, and then we headed back to the start of the hiking trail.

When we got back, we finally had some food, and Tamara started following the peacock again. She got so close and personal with it that other tourists started taking pictures of her! It seemed kind of funny that this woman had become part of the tourist attraction itself. I was immediately reminded of a similar experience in New York City, where she was feeding French fries to a squirrel, which started eating them out of her hand. Other tourists were taking photos of her feeding the squirrel. But here in Hawaii, we headed back to the hotel, relaxed, and went to bed early as the next day would be an early one.

One of the biggest things about this trip was to ensure that we had a lot of free time. Since our other vacations had typically been so busy, it was essential in making sure that we didn't have a lot on our plate for this trip. For the seven days that we spent there, only two of them had organized touring. The first of those two tours was from Discover Hawaii, where we would get a chance to go over to Big Island and see the volcano at Mt. Kilauea. That tour started bright and early on Monday morning.

We got picked up at the hotel and shuttled back to the airport, where we took an early morning flight to Big Island. Once we were picked up at the Hilo airport, the sightseeing began.

If you put this book down and go Google "banyan trees," you'll immediately notice that these things aren't like any regular trees you have back home. So, the tour started with a little drive and stopped at Banyan Drive.

This street, known locally as the "Hilo Walk of Fame," is a tree-lined street in Hilo that is literally just a series of banyan trees along the road. The trees line the motorway and are also visible in the nearby park. For me, this was my first experience seeing these trees in the real world. Before that, my only knowledge of banyan trees was what I saw on the TV show LOST. The trees themselves are pretty impressive, but what struck me the most is how dense they are. I never really thought much of trees in general, but these were quite a sight to see.

We walked around the area, took a bunch of photos, and I was even able to find a geocache located almost beside the bus we were on. Before we knew it, it was time to move along to the next location: Punalu'u Black Sand Beach.

As the name suggests, the sand on this beach is black. And when I say it's black, I mean it's really black. It's as black as charcoal. I picked some of the sand up and ran it through my fingers. It didn't even feel like sand at all. Having spent plenty of time at the beach, I know what sand is supposed to feel like, but this certainly didn't feel like beach sand. Turns out, it's an entirely different kind of formation process than typical beach sand.

The islands of Hawaii are an extensive archipelago that was formed by volcanos under the seawater. When the volcano erupts or emits magma from its core, it is immediately cooled and hardens into rock. As the eruptions on the seafloor continue to erupt magma, more and more land mass is created. This is where all of the Hawaiian and other types of islands have come from. As previously noted, Galapagos is another example.

The black beach sand forms the same way. The magma from the earth is hardened by the water, but instead of remaining solid, it cracks and splits into tiny little particles and forms black sand. When you pick up a handful of this stuff, it doesn't have the grainy feel like typical beach sand and feels more like a handful of rock salt.

When Tamara and I visited the Dead Sea in Jordan, we took a walk along the beach until we got to an area where some salt sands could be scooped up. Tamara had brought a couple of small little vials to bring some of the sand home. Her plan was to do the same thing in Hawaii for some of the beach sand there.

During our tour, the guide told us the story of Pele, the Hawaiian Goddess of Fire. The legend goes that she created all of the islands herself. Anyone who removes any of the natural parts of the islands would be cursed by Pele. The guide told us many stories of people who took sand or rocks from Hawaii and had horrible things happen to them after returning to the mainland. In fact, he recounted a story of someone who returned something to Hawaii in hopes of relinquishing the bad luck he had acquired after taking sand from a beach on the islands. Apparently, after replacing the sand and going home, all his bad luck faded away.

Despite the warning, my wife opted to bring home a little of that black sand with her. I won't discount the possibility of bad luck, but so far, so good on our side.

After leaving the beach, we were dropped off at Big Island Candies while the driver returned to the airport to pick up a few other tourists. The layover was only about an hour, so we checked the place out, and I went out and snagged a geocache across the street. Before we knew it, we were on our way again. Next stop: Rainbow Falls.

Rainbow Falls is aptly named. The volume of water coming over the edge causes a thick spray to develop. The mist forms a rainbow along the falls itself, so on a sunny day, the rainbow is clearly visible from the top of the falls. We stood there at the lookout point and just looked at the falls. When people describe Hawaii as being a paradise or the closest thing to Eden on earth, I imagine they are talking about a place like this. The natural beauty here was pretty awe-inspiring, but at the same time, there was a part of me that wished I could jump off the falls into the pool below. Yet again, the daredevil in me wanted to come out and play.

After checking out the view, we wandered around the area for a little while, snapped some photos, buried ourselves in a few banyan trees, and then headed out again. It was time to get to the main attraction on this tour of Big Island: the volcano.

Since the entire island itself literally sits on a volcano, the main reason people come to this island for the first time is to see the volcano itself. What is a little harder to fathom is that it really is all over the place. From one part of the island to another, remnants of the volcano's destructive power can be seen.

On Big Island, the Hawaii Volcanoes National Park covers a nice portion of the southeastern part of the island. The tour we took spent pretty much the rest of the day going in and around this national park.

Along one road, dubbed the "Chain of Craters" road, the forest area was black and hardened from the magma that had covered the entire region. Looking out the window from the bus, you'd see a thick forest whizzing by as we drove, then as if someone flipped a switch, all the trees would disappear, and all you would notice is black everywhere. It looked like black tar was covering the entire landscape. Instead of your view being blocked by trees, everything was completely open, with almost nothing growing out of it. All you could see in any direction was black magma that had hardened. Then as fast as it appeared, the trees would start up again. This pattern emerged all throughout the island.

I remember thinking as we drove through those dead areas that the region felt almost alien to me. In fact, I thought of the movie Interstellar as we drove by. In the film, they land on an ice planet, and I remember thinking that in a way, this whole region reminded me of that planet except everything was black, not white. It's as close as I had come to being in an area that felt genuinely alien to me. Forest fire destruction had nothing on what the lava did to the land here.

The guide told us that the volcano had erupted in certain spots and covered the actual road. We made a stop along the way where a detour road had been created because the old road had been covered by hardened lava. You could see the asphalt like on a normal road. Then it was just cut off by the remnants of the volcanic lava flow that went over it. I stood in the middle of a former street that was only about 75 feet long but book-ended by hardened lava on either side. I remember taking many photos and being in complete disbelief about there being a road buried under all of that lava. The guide told us that it had only been a few years since that part of the street had been destroyed, and that lava flows were common to see. This was long before the eruption and lava flows in 2018.

Along Crater Rim Drive, we got two particularly incredible views. The first one was of the "steam vents." These vents have been exposed to show off the steam that was underneath the ground. The vents, or holes, allow the steam to be "vented" to the open air. The bus stopped at a small little area where there was nothing but a small 10'x 3' hole in the ground. Anywhere else, it would have just looked like some service repair guy had dug a big hole to work on an underground power line. That wasn't the case here. A hot steady stream of steam was coming out of the vent. The tour guide told everyone that they'd get the best facial from the steam.

The hole represented a vent chamber by which the heat from the underground volcano vents upwards and out to the open air. There were several spots in this area where you could see the steam, and in the distance, you could see more steam rising up. When you put your hand over it, the mist wasn't hot enough to burn you, but it was certainly enough for you to feel it and sweat it. I snapped a photo of Tamara, who had put her head down as far as she could, and when she came up, her glasses were fogged up.

Not far from there, we got a good view of the actual caldera itself. A caldera is a fancy word for a giant crater. We didn't drive into it, but you could clearly see it from where we were. There were plenty of hiking trails where one could actually hike down into the crater and get closer to the real thing. Looking at it from afar really didn't give much perspective on what it actually was. What was more enticing was the idea that under that crater, there was a volcano.

The last major thing for us to visit before we made our way to see the lava flows was a visit to the Thurston Lava Tube. Now the lava tube itself was probably the most impressive part of my volcano tour.

Lava tubes are naturally occurring tunnels that get created underground by moving lava. If you have ever gone through a manmade shaft, a lava tube is very similar. We drill and bore our way through the rock to create the tunnel; a lava tube is produced by naturally flowing lava through the rock that cools on its edge to form a tunnel or tube. Also similar to how ants bore tunnels through dirt, except, in this case, the shafts are made with lava.

This tube was about 600 feet long and between 10 and 30 feet high, depending on the area. It's also speculated to be about 400 years old.

The walk through the tunnel was pretty cool. Previous to the tour, I knew we would be going through the tube, so I brought a flashlight with me. The idea that lava itself had eaten away the rock and created the tube made this place even more alluring. Some people were scared to go into the tunnel, but for me, it was just another hole in the ground. Definitely, a must-see if visiting Big Island for the first time.

Our last, and sadly most disappointing, stop of the day was at an area designed to showcase the actual lava flows itself. The stop, located near the Jaggar museum, is left to the very end, at nighttime, so that you can see the glow of the lava below easily. It had been a rainy and foggy day for almost the entire afternoon. That turned into a fog that evening. There was absolutely no way to see any kind of lava flow from this spot, given the weather conditions. The tour guide felt really bad as he indicated the fog usually lifts during the evenings, but it wasn't meant to be.

I really wanted to see the lava flows themselves. We stayed as long as we could, but eventually, the tour guide wrangled us all together back on the bus, and it was time to take off. Before I knew it, I was sitting on a plane, and then again in my bedroom. The first of two tours completed.

The next day was an open day. We could do pretty much anything we wanted, so we took the advice of one of my friends and opted to drive up and see the Dole plantation where they grow and harvest pineapple. It was only an hour or so away by car, and given that the cost was pretty cheap, it made for an easy little excursion.

We arrived there, and sure enough, there were plenty of people already checking the place out. There's a pretty significant "store" where you can buy pretty much anything related to pineapples or other Dole products. I actually picked up some hot sauce for my father-in-law and perused through the whole store.

Within about 30 minutes, I was already kind of bored. Tamara and I opted to go for a nice walk through the gardens and then hopped on the little train ride that takes you way out into the plantation. The trip itself was ok, but the lineup and organization for it were not. I'm sure we must have stood there in line for almost an hour while we waited to get on what was mostly a kiddie ride through the back of the plantation.

The only notable things about our visit to the plantation were the pineapple display session and my adventures in finding a geocache in the middle of many plants.

The pineapple display was a local taking a pineapple and showed us how to properly open it, cut it, and serve it. The whole process didn't take very long, but it was pretty cool to watch, and we got to have fresh pineapple. It wasn't as "popping" as I thought it would be, but because of the time of year, pineapples weren't in season, so they weren't as fresh as they would have been otherwise.

I did spend a little bit of time in the middle of the plantation, trying to find a geocache. I had spotted one on the map and went looking for it, but no matter how hard I tried, I couldn't find it. My wife even wanted to help me, and after what felt like forever, we managed to find the container which ended up being hidden in plain sight within a nicely camouflaged bottle. I am sure there were plenty of people looking at the both of us, wondering what we were doing. It was pretty entertaining.

The rest of the day was all about exploring the beaches along the North Shore and getting some snorkeling opportunities. Ever since we had been to the Red Sea in Jordan, Tamara had become quite enamored with snorkeling. We knew that we'd spend a considerable amount of time doing some while in Hawaii.

We did a bunch of research to try and find the best spots to go snorkeling. Hanauma Bay is listed as probably the best (and it pretty much was), but it's also the busiest. We knew we wanted to try it out while we were in town, but many places listed both Sharks Cove and Three Tables as great spots to go snorkeling. These beach areas were pretty close together and are just north of the Waimea Valley while driving along the coast. We parked the car and made our way down, and before we knew it, we were face down in the water, exploring everywhere.

Both of these spots were covered in rock formations and coral. The water, for the most part, is actually pretty shallow (a couple of feet), so you had to be careful where you steered yourself. You'd go one direction and spot a ton of bright fish and then turn around another way, and you'd find even more to see. Just when you thought you'd had enough, you'd spot something else and then end up kicking or bumping into someone else who had found the same thing. Not a lot of people, but the areas for snorkeling were pretty popular.

Sharks Cove was really close, so we just walked over and then got in the water. The beautiful thing about the cove was that it was surrounded by rocks, which provided natural protection from the high waves of the sea. This made the snorkeling area really calm and ripe for viewing. We spent a considerable amount of time weaving in and out of the various rocks and coral spots around here. I'm sure we must have been there for at least a couple of hours. Tamara was doing her best to try and spot a sea turtle as that was what she really wanted to encounter. No turtles this time around, but there were plenty of fish and other sea creatures to snap photos of.

That particular day we saw a lot of wave activity as the water crashed against the rocks and splashed upwards. In some cases, you'd hear a loud BANG and then turn around and see water flying everywhere. Some people were walking along the edges of the rocks that separated the cove from the open ocean. I stood there and watched as huge splashes of water crashed into the rocks and wondered how long it would take before one of those people fell over. No one ever did, and I was tempted to try it but chose not to. I could see how dangerous the water there really was. Tamara would get her own taste of that later.

Another subtle side effect of the rocks and water is that in some cases, you'd see the water trickle down through the rock formation creating a small little waterfall. Nothing like what we had seen earlier in the week, but still pretty cool to spot.

I'd had my fill of the water, so I got out and dried off while the wife kept at it for a little longer. Before we knew it, the sun was setting, and it was time to call it a day. Tomorrow would be LOST day.

Knowing that I wanted to keep the touring down while in Hawaii, there was only one other thing I wanted to do. As a huge TV addict, the show LOST sits near the top of television shows I was a massive fan of. Most of the show was shot on the island of Oahu in Hawaii. When I knew we were going there for a trip, I started digging for LOST themed tours and found the perfect tour from KOS Tours. They do a full tour of the entire island all by a hummer, and I was psyched to finally see some of these spots from the show.

Again, we got picked up at our hotel, met our tour guide, and away we went. Honestly, this tour was probably my favorite part of the trip. Not only did I get a chance to visit all of these places used by the show, but we got a really in-depth look at much of the island in a way that we would never have otherwise seen it.

If you don't know anything about the TV show LOST, some of this may go over your head.

The tour actually started in Honolulu. We took a gander at Hurley's house and drove by a TV studio where some interior shots were done for parts of the show. As we left the city, we started around the island in a counterclockwise fashion. We left Honolulu, and our guide told us that Josh Holloway, who played Sawyer, owned a home in Oahu and pointed at the area where he lived. Tamara was tempted to see if we could find his house the following day when we went for our own drive, but we opted to just go exploring on our own.

The first notable spot outside the city was a beautiful lookout point called Lanai Lookout. This lookout point was used many times throughout the life of the series. Most notably, it was used as the location where Desmond confronts Kelvin and kills him and when Jack and Locke have their final fight in the series finale. I snapped a ton of pictures from here not only because of the use of the spot in the show (I have a photo of me standing where Locke & Jack fought), but the view of the bay was pretty unique from that spot. What was even more impressive was that our guide had brought an iPad with screengrabs from various episodes, including those that were shot here. He would hold the iPad up and use the ocean and rocks as a backdrop comparison. He also showed how they mixed both the real and not so real into the show to make these scenes look as they did. In some cases, entire shorelines and backgrounds were digitally replaced. In other instances, the natural beauty of the island was enough.

From that lookout point, we continued counterclockwise around the island of Oahu. There were plenty of little stops here and there as we drove along the shoreline. We stopped at several locations along the west coast, including Moli' I Pond, where the Dharma dock was and the Byodo-In Temple where Sun & Jin got married. We actually spent about 30 minutes or so at the temple and got some really great pictures. It's a gorgeous spot and definitely worth the visit whether you are a fan of the show or not.

Halfway through the tour, we took a minor break to pay our bill at a visitor's stop located at the entrance to the Kualoa Ranch. This is a private ranch in Oahu that is very well known for its use in movies. Pretty much anytime you saw the folks from LOST wandering through a "valley" or large greenery area, it was on this ranch. Most of the vast fields where you saw dinosaurs roaming free in Jurassic Park were also shot on this same property. You can take a tour of the ranch itself, but we opted to just keep on moving and get closer to the North Shore, where even more sights would be seen.

Shortly after leaving the ranch, our guide told us that the new King Kong movie was currently being shot on the ranch. He said if you looked closely enough, you could see little yellow signs with black text on them posted to power poles with arrows on them. They were intended to guide folks involved in the film shoot to where the actual filming was taking place. As we drove a bit further, we passed what he referred to as the "private entrance/back door" of the ranch, and sure enough, there was a little yellow sign on the pole with an arrow pointing straight in. I would have loved to have seen something being shot there, but alas, no luck today.

Eventually, we hit the North Shore, where we had already

spent some time exploring on our own, but this was all LOST themed. We stopped at a small little grocery store and picked up some food for lunch. The tour included dropping us off at Papailoa Beach, where Tamara and I would have our own private little picnic right on Losties beach. The beach seen in LOST seasons 3-6 was shot right there.

Tamara's feet were pretty sore, but I was all revved up. This was one of two locations on this tour that I wanted to see the most. I got right up to where Sawyer's tent was propped up and took a ton of photos of the area. Yeah, it was pretty cheezy to be that "fan-boyish" over something like a beach from a TV show, but I didn't care. I was really enjoying being on that beach. Plus, let's face it; I was in Hawaii and its pretty much heaven there.

We chowed down some food, headed back to the car, and eventually got picked up by our tour guide who took us to our final location: Camp Erdman.

This outdoor camp is owned by the local YMCA, but for LOST fans, you'd know this location as Dharmaville. All of the little houses from the show are original buildings used by the camp regularly. The show simply borrowed them to film all of the Dharma exterior shots. We started in one of the main rooms they used for the "orientation" day shots, and Tamara posed for a photo where "Kate" had been. We then crossed the street to find all of the little "houses" from Dharmaville.

This was the second location that I was excited about, and in retrospect, my favorite. I was in my glory wandering around the little "houses," snapping pictures, and just reveling at the moment. I sat in a chair in front of the "house" that Ben lived in and had Tamara take a photo of me that was very close in resemblance to one of the shots from the show.

Our guide had actually done a similar shot on the first beach we visited by getting me to sit on a log. He held up an action figure of Charlie from the show and got Tamara to take a forced perspective photo of me. The picture made it look like I was sitting on the log with Charlie. Unfortunately, by the time I got back to the hotel later that day, all the photos from my phone were lost when the phone died. Thankfully our regular camera shots all came out, including the one of me sitting in Ben's chair in front of his house.

Just shortly before heading back to the car, I dug out my GPS and looked, and sure enough, there was a geocache just across the street. It was a quick and easy find, and then that was it for the tour. He drove us back to Waikiki and pointed out a couple of other little spots in the area, including the bar that Sawyer met Jack's dad in. Turns out, it was actually walking distance from our hotel. We pondered going there for supper but opted for the Outback instead. By the end of that day, we were exhausted but quite content by what we had seen.

The next day was going to be our last full day while in Hawaii, as we were leaving in the evening on Friday, so we wanted to make the best of it. We had done some snorkeling here and there in a few places but had been told that the best place in Oahu to go snorkeling was Hanauma Bay. We lucked out because that particular day was Thanksgiving in the US, which meant that most touristy areas would not be as busy as others. We got up bright and early and went down to get some snorkeling done as we wanted to spend as much of the day there as we could.

And we did. That day was all in the bay.

We must have burned through several GoPro batteries shooting a ton of footage and taking pictures of the countless fish and wildlife we saw in the area. Some of the coral areas were pretty shallow, so you had to be careful of making sure you didn't scratch or cut yourself on the coral itself. I'd learned that the hard way in the Red Sea, where I got a mild infection from the coral. We also learned very quickly that the current and waves of the water there are not to be messed with. They had a recommended area that people were to snorkel in, but it wasn't against the law or even the local rules to go beyond that.

Tamara and I tried to swim out a bit further in hopes of seeing a sea turtle or two as we had heard they liked the area. We looked and looked but never managed to spot one. What we did come up with was being pulled a bit further away from shore than we were comfortable. I remember looking back at the beach and wondering how I had gotten so far away from it. I had to take a beat before working my way back as I could feel myself getting a little panicky. Before long, I was back closer to the beach and opted to take a short break. We did manage to use the GoPro to take a pretty cool underwater selfie, which I had made into a crystal ornament for our anniversary.

While the wife did a ton more snorkeling, I went exploring around the park area itself. There were several geocaches in the area, and I wanted to try and find them, plus I just wanted to see what else was there. I snapped a couple of pictures of some birds and a mongoose. I then kicked back and enjoyed the view of the bay from the top.

By the time I went back down, Tamara had migrated to a completely different part of the bay, so I spent a reasonable amount of time trying to find her. Eventually, when she came up for air, I spotted her and then headed back to our little spot in the sand. Before we knew it, we were heading back to the hotel and getting ready to pack.

We got up the following morning and did a mini-tour of the hotel grounds itself. With all the island exploring we had done, we hadn't bothered to really check out the resort. We wandered around quite a bit, snapping photos of the landscape artwork, the buildings themselves, and countless palm trees. Alas, eventually, we had to check out and find something to keep ourselves occupied for the day. For us, that was a return trip to the North Shore, but not for more snorkeling this time. I had turned the TV on to a surfing competition going on up there. We figured we could see that and enjoy the beach one last time before we headed back home.

By the time we got there, most of the surfing action had already finished, and it was just mainly spectators watching some of the surfer's practice. We parked our car and headed out to a beach, which was marked by a huge tent that read "The Vans World Cup of Surfing." Sitting on the beach, we enjoyed the view, watched the surfers, and then my wife decided to pull a stunt that would make our last day very memorable.

We watched a couple of kids go out on little boards and get pulled and pushed by the waves. These aren't the small waves of Parlee Beach that we are used to. These are real waves with a natural pull and undertows that have the power to suck you in and eat you up alive. As adventurous as I can be, I didn't want to go anywhere near them. My wife on the other hand…

She opted to go down to the water and let the waves crash into her. She stood on the edge of the shoreline as one of these giant waves came closer and closer. I had my camera out, so I started snapping pictures because I knew damn well, she would fall over flat on her ass. As the first wave hit her, I heard a woman off to my left say something to the effect of "She's going to get herself killed." The second wave hit, and sure enough, flat on her back, she went. Another wave crashed over the top of her before she could get up, and although I knew she was ok and in no real danger, others around didn't feel the same way. By the time I stood up, a lifeguard had jumped down and run over to her to make sure she was ok. She laughed her ass off, telling him she was fine as he helped her to her feet, and she walked back over to me.

I have a series of several photos in sequential order that tell the story of her almost getting sucked out to sea. Every time we see or hear anything about surfers at a beach, that experience comes up in conversation. That was pretty much the end of our Hawaii trip. She got dried off, headed back to the jeep, and went straight to the airport. An overnight flight to Vancouver, then to Toronto, and back to Moncton, we got home a little after midnight on Saturday.

In some ways, Hawaii stands out as a memorable vacation for a very different reason than many other places I have visited. It doesn't jump out at me as being a place as historically spectacular as some of the other locations I have been to. However, I will say that when people say that visiting Hawaii "changes you" and that you want to go back, they aren't lying. There really is something about that place that seems to want to draw you back. For me, I think it's the fact that it combines a bit of the familiar with a bit of the foreign, all in one location. So, for those who want to get away, but don't want to completely walk away from what they know, Hawaii is definitely the place to visit.

Spend Your Life Living,
Not Having

When I end up in conversations with people about my travels, there are two questions I get asked more than anything.

"What was your favorite place to visit?"

"Where are you going to go next?"

It's actually pretty easy to pick the places I have enjoyed the most. Of all of the settings I have been fortunate enough to visit, Jordan still stands out amongst them all as being probably my most memorable. There was just something so foreign and unexpected about that place. It always sticks out in my mind as being at the top of my list. Australia and Africa would also rate high up as well. As for what comes next, well, that's a different story.

There are seven continents in the world, and I have been to six of them. I can't help but feel like that seventh continent is just taunting me to go visit. I'd love to put Antarctica on my list of places I have been to, but at the end of the day, that's a trip that costs a lot of money, and I don't know if it's one I am ready to try and take on. Plus, I hate the cold. Why would I want to spend more than 10K on a trip to go somewhere where the temperature is that cold? Well, you go because you want to see what you can't see anywhere else. So maybe one day I will find a way to make it there. Until then, I have some other, more accessible spots to visit.

I'd love to go to a country like northern Norway or Finland during the time of year when the sun doesn't set, or the sun never rises. Parts of Alaska are known to have 67 days of nighttime, which to me, is absolutely unfathomable. What would it be like to be in a place where at 12 noon, it's nighttime? I'd love to go to bed at midnight and look out my window and still see the sun shining. I'll never make it to Mars, so I think being in a place where the sunrise and sunset are missing would be as close to an alien world as I would ever get the chance to visit.

I've heard Thailand is pretty amazing. I have several colleagues who swear by it and say that if I have the chance to go, I should.

The famous statues on Easter Island in South America or the Angkor Wat temple in Cambodia are a couple of other spots I'd love to see. A few friends of mine have done the hike of Machu Picchu and said it was also quite impressive. Visiting the ancient city would be pretty incredible, but I don't know if I'd be up to the hike itself.

The town can be accessed without doing the walk, but that sort of defeats the purpose of going there.

China, Japan, Fiji, and maybe a return trip to Australia would be enjoyable as well. I've also thought of taking a flight to Paris or London and then just trying to find my own way across a dozen or so countries. I don't have a lot of ambition to experience much of the history of that part of the world, but I do think it would be pretty sweet to at least see some of it before my time expires.

I'd love to be able to make one of those "trips around the world," where I take a couple of weeks and fly from country to country and wrap the entire globe. Like Antarctica, it's a costly trip to make, but it would be one hell of a great story to tell. This, of course, brings me to the entire point of all of my travel.

In 1995, I took my first real "vacation" somewhere. Since then, between work and pleasure, I've traveled over 600,000 kilometers across 19 different countries. I've seen my share of famous landmarks and even met the odd celebrity here and there. I've snapped thousands of photos that will never honestly describe what it was like to be there in the moment. I've enjoyed the food, friendship, and family of many people I have met along my journey. From all of that, I have learned one fundamental lesson.

Spend your life living, not having.

Those six words have become my own personal mantra these last few years, and the more I think about them, the more I realize how true they really are.

So many people do anything and everything they can to acquire stuff. Cars, homes, jewels, technology, and many other status symbols fill their life with a bunch of "stuff." In the end, what happens to all of that "stuff"? The moment you buy it, it's already outdated. Something new and flashier always comes along to replace it and remind you that you again need to get more "stuff." With all the money in the world, having all of that stuff won't actually give you a "full" life. But experiences, those never get old, and they never change.

When I turn 80 years old, I'll be telling my grandchildren about me jumping off the Stratosphere Tower in Las Vegas. Their eyes will widen when I tell them about elephants eating the tree outside my treehouse in Africa. My friends and family will laugh when I talk about being mugged by a seagull in Australia. Others will stand still and listen to me tell the story of watching a baby sea turtle scurry frantically to the ocean to avoid being captured by wild birds. Those experiences will stay with me for life. No matter how much time passes or how much my life changes, all of the memories and experiences of going out and just "doing it" will be with me. And if I happen to lose my recollection of some of those experiences, I can always open this book up and read about them.

It doesn't matter whether you have a million dollars or only one dollar. Every person should be doing what they can to "live" their life and not just be alive. Spend the time you have in your life, embracing new experiences and seeing anything and everything you can. Because at the end of your life, when you look back, you won't regret what you did. You'll regret what you didn't do. Today, I have no regrets.

THE END

APPENDIX I

Mugged by Seagulls, The Video

If you'd like to see a "visual" representation of the stories from this book, please feel free to check out a little music video I made. It includes a lot of footage from the locations discussed in this book.

https://matthewklem.com/index.php/seagullsvideo/

The Other Africa Story

After this book was written, I made another trip to Africa to visit Victoria Falls. I wrote a nice article about the that trek on my travel blog. It includes photos and videos of what I experienced there.

https://bit.ly/3iXrhzH

CPSIA information can be obtained
at www.ICGtesting.com
Printed in the USA
LVHW082014280921
698935LV00010B/294